Disney
Recipes

From Animation
to Inspiration

Recipes by Ira L. Meyer
Edited by Marcello Garofalo
Graphic design: Raimondo Monti
Editorial Staff: Epierre - Milano (Mi)
Language consultant: John Rugman
Photographs: Fiorenza Cicogna
Food stylist: Corrado Calza
Cover design by Elliot Kreloff
Back cover photo of Ira L. Meyer: Richard Lee

Mushu's Egg Rolls and Juk; Mulan's Mahogany Chicken: Adapted from Walt Disney Pictures' *Mulan*
Music by Matthew Wilder. Lyrics by David Zippel
Original Score by Jerry Goldsmith. Produced by Pam Coats
Directed by Barry Cook and Tony Bancroft

Philoctetes' Onion Marmalade with Raisins; Heroes' Herculade: Adapted from Walt Disney Pictures' *Hercules*
Music by Alan Menken. Lyrics by David Zippel
Original score by Alan Menken. Produced by Alice Dewey and John Musker & Ron Clements
Directed by John Musker & Ron Clements.

All Tarzan materials © 2003 Edgar Rice Burroughs, Inc., and Disney Enterprises, Inc.
All Rights Reserved. TARZAN® Owned by Edgar Rice Burroughs, Inc. and Used by Permission.

101 Dalmatians is based on the book by Dodie Smith, published by Viking Press.

Winnie the Pooh characters based on the "Winnie the Pooh" works by A. A. Milne and E.H. Shepard.

Walt Disney's *Bambi* is based on the original story by Felix Salten.

Dumbo is based on the Walt Disney motion picture, *Dumbo*, suggested by the story *Dumbo, the flying elephant*, by Helen Aberson and Harold Perl.
Copyright 1939 by Rollabook Publishers.

Mary Poppins is based on the Walt Disney motion picture, *Mary Poppins*, based on the series of books by P. L. Travers.

All material featuring characters from the Disney films *The Rescuers/The Rescuers Down Under*
suggested by the books by Margery Sharp, *The Rescuers* and *Miss Bianca*, published by Little, Brown and Company

Kanine Krunchies Kommercial: Words and Music by Mel Leven
© 1959 Wonderland Music Company, Inc. (BMI)

Les Poissons: Words by Howard Ashman
Music by Alan Menken © 1988 Walt Disney Music Company (ASCAP) and Wonderland Music Company, Inc. (BMI)

Walrus and the Carpenter: Words by Bob Hilliard
Music by Sammy Fain © 1949 Walt Disney Music Company (ASCAP)

Disney Editions Editorial Director: Wendy Lefkon
Disney Editions Editor: Jody Revenson
Disney Editions Design Manager: Paul W. Banks

For information address Disney Editions, 114 Fifth Avenue, New York, New York 10011-5690.
www.disneyeditions.com

Library of Congress Cataloging-in-Publication Data on file.

ISBN: 0-7868-5416-2

Printed in Italy

First Edition

10 9 8 7 6 5 4 3 2 1

*The publisher would like to thank Colavita Pasta and
Colavita Olive Oil for their contribution to the creation of this book.*

DISNEY RECIPES

From Animation to Inspiration

Recipes by Ira L. Meyer

Edited by Marcello Garofalo

DISNEY EDITIONS

NEW YORK

TABLE OF CONTENTS

TABLE OF CONTENTS

▉ BAKED GOODS

▉ DRINKS

> **I THINK ALL ARTISTS — WHETHER THEY PAINT, WRITE, SING OR PLAY MUSIC, WRITE FOR THE THEATER OR MOVIES, MAKE POETRY OR SCULPTURE — ALL OF THESE ARE FIRST OF ALL PLEASURE GIVERS.**
>
> —*WALT DISNEY*

Walt began with a dream, which he turned into a new form of life: animation. For this very special book of recipes I have built upon some of his visionary thoughts and ideas. Usually, chefs begin with raw materials and combine them to create wonderful dishes. My first approach, however, was to imagine what kind of hidden taste memories were bubbling inside the heads of the Disney animators as they created the characters and scenes we all know and love. I would also venture to say that even behind the sketches and scenes that never made it to celluloid, there was the idea of a dish—a filling and comforting food to be placed before someone to enjoy. I became a detective of sorts, researching and reading, tasting and observing, determining which foods the Disney characters might enjoy or actually do eat in the films and cartoon shorts in which they appear. Indeed, creating real food from animation has been a serious and fun endeavor, and I like to think of myself as a pleasure giver, in the mold of Walt Disney himself. Is this art imitating life or life imitating art? I'll leave it to you to decide. What I am sure of is that these recipes taste good and give me the same warm feeling I had as a child when I left a Saturday afternoon matinee, fully satisfied.

—Ira L. Meyer

"**I LOVE A STORY
WITH FOOD IN IT.** "

*Einstein, the Great Dane
of* Oliver & Company

"**M**y gold, my kingdom for a hamburger sandwich!" pleads King Midas in *The Golden Touch*, one of the rare Silly Symphony cartoons that Walt Disney himself directed. Food has been portrayed in cinema, including animated features and shorts, ever since the medium began. On the big screen, food plays a variety of roles and serves different purposes—as a focal point in social settings and conflicts, as accompaniment to breaks in the action and characters' existential reflections, as a prelude to romance or tragedy, and very often as a cue for comic situations or responses.

As long as movies and life reflect each other, then animation will be linked to both. This is a crucial point in understanding the workings of the world of Disney, where food symbolism has played a crucial role. A host of characters is seen in the act of making or tasting, a soup, a cake, a roast, or some other delicious dish. Even if we only considered the first Disney feature film, *Snow White and the Seven Dwarfs*, an authentic and unrepeatable compendium of cinematic genres, we realize that a bowl of soup becomes a pretext for social interaction—and eventually conflict—among the characters, while a gooseberry pie is a prelude to tragedy—to say nothing of the "special treatment" afforded a certain apple. Also common are food interludes, filling the gap during breaks in the action, while they become unforgettable moments in and of themselves.

The importance of food in the history of cinema is glaringly clear. In *Gone with the Wind* (1938, directed by Victor Fleming), in the scene before the ball, Mammy, while lacing up Scarlett's corset, advises her not to leave the house on an empty stomach: "Miz Scarlett, young ladies should eat like birds at parties. Before you go, eat some of my muffins." As Humphrey Bogart and Ingrid Bergman embark upon their passion-filled love story at Rick's Café Americain in *Casablanca* (1942, directed by Michael Curtiz), with "As Time

Goes By" playing in the background, the two sip cocktails and munch on tuna canapés. In *Citizen Kane* (1941, directed by Orson Welles), Kane treats his friends and collaborators to a splendid banquet that serves to punctuate a change of heart in the main character.

In Disney films, too, food placates, encourages, consoles, and inspires. In *Beauty and the Beast,* Lumiere offers Belle—just before she must once again face the ire of the enraged Beast—a tray of tasty treats, suggesting she try the gray stuff, which is delicious. And if she doesn't believe him she can ask the dishes! In *The Rescuers Down Under*, the two wayward mice wind up inside a fancy restaurant—Miss Bianca is wearing

a broad-brimmed hat just like Ingrid Bergman's in *Casablanca*— where champagne toasts detour a would-be love story and lead the lovable little creatures to an unexpected adventure. In a memorable scene from *Sleeping Beauty*, King Hubert holds a sumptuous feast to celebrate with his future in-law King Stefan the political union of their respective kingdoms, a food break designed to underscore a historic, family-centered transformation.

There are basically three ways to introduce a meal in a film: food may appear on the screen, be mentioned, or simply be alluded to. Disney artists applied such criteria in *Pinocchio*, where Figaro the cat anticipates a succulent trout prepared by Geppetto, as both wait in vain for the return of their favorite puppet for dinner; in the short movie *The Three Little Wolves*, the Big Bad Wolf comments to his children the exquisiteness of pork; in *Song of the South*, Br'er Fox and Br'er Bear have their hearts set on a bowl of soup or roast rabbit, which, alas, they never get to taste. Food philosophy is

prevalent in the world of Disney: in *The Jungle Book* Baloo sings
proudly about the bare necessities being Mother Nature's recipes;
Mary Poppins chirps that a spoonful of sugar helps the medicine go down;
in *Aladdin*, the Genie claims that life is his master's restaurant
and he's the maitre d'; while in *The Lion King*, for Timon, inventor of
"hakuna matata," adaptation is the cornerstone of his outlook—even with
regard food, as he reminds Simba.

Practicality is just as important to the Wise Old Owl in *So Dear to My
Heart*, who maintains that "It's what you do with what you got that counts!"
This has become a dictum of professional and amateur chefs alike.

In the short movie *Mickey's Trailer,* Mickey does his best to serve a
complete breakfast to friends Goofy and Donald Duck—fresh milk and corn
on the cob from nearby farms, with coffee, potatoes, and watermelon. In *The
Little Mermaid,* chef Louis churns out a series of tasty seafood dishes
(including his specialty, stuffed crab), and Sebastian makes a narrow escape
from the kitchen; in *Treasure Planet,* John Silver slices and fries up alien
forms of fish, coelenterates, and gasteropods for what we can only imagine is
a tasty extraterrestrial supper. In *Atlantis: The Lost Empire* Cookie prepares
the same energetic and essential meal of lard, bacon, and beans—day in,
and day out for the brawny crew. Kronk, Yzma's stolid assistant in *The
Emperor's New Groove*, organizes an entire dinner consisting of soup, a light
salad, spinach puffs, coffee, and dessert, in order to offer His Majesty a
poison-laced cocktail. Food is a common denominator for tragedy and
parody: Goofy, in *Mickey's Birthday Party*, and Fauna, in *Sleeping Beauty*, are

both asking for trouble as they prepare multilayer cakes, while in *Chef Donald*, the star of the show attempts to make pancakes following instructions broadcast over the radio—unfortunately, he unwittingly spills rubber cement into the batter. Some fools have all the luck, it seems: the Mad Hatter and the March Hare pull cakes from their hats to celebrate the "unbirthdays" of Alice and the Queen of Hearts, and even spread butter and jam on their wristwatches ("*Muthtard?!* Don't let'th be *thilly!*") as they slurp cup after cup of tea.

The eccentric star of *The Reluctant Dragon* eats breakfast off his belly and composes an ode to an upside-down cake. A starving

Donald Duck clearly goes off the deep end in *Fun and Fancy Free* when he sinks his beak into a piece of porcelain dinnerware, an almost extreme homage to the scene in Charlie Chaplin's *The Gold Rush* (1925), in which the Tramp boils and attempts to eat a shoe. Lost in her Wonderland, Alice is truly at a gastronomic loss when she bites into carrots and licks mysterious mushrooms that change her size. Further evidence is her opinion of the super shrinking drink she tastes: "Mmm . . . Tastes like . . . cherry tart. Custard. Pineapple. Roast turkey. . . ." And consider restaurant owner Mudka, who in *The Emperors's New Groove* serves up "two heartburns . . . and a deep-fried doorstop" to Kuzco and Pacha.

Treating guests properly is another big theme. One of the grandest hosts in the Disney cavalcade is surely Lumiere, as he offers Belle the menu and ushers in a phantasmagoric Busby Berkeley–style show never before seen in a cartoon. Not to be outdone, Tony and Joe prepare their legendary Spaghetti and Meatballs for the love-struck stars of *Lady and the Tramp*. Rabbit, however, seems somewhat put out when Winnie the Pooh shows up for dinner. To Rabbit's hesitating query, "Would you like condensed milk . . . or honey on your bread?" the cuddly bear's response is emblematic: "Both! But never mind the bread, please." Ariel feels just as uncomfortable at Eric's castle, both because of her "improper" use of the fork and because of Sebastian's shenanigans as he seeks refuge on her plate. The pretty little mermaid's clumsiness inspired Julia Roberts's battle with a snail *à la bourguignonne* in *Pretty Woman* (1990, directed by Garry Marshall).

On the other hand, some guests may not receive such warm welcomes. In the 1918 short *The Cook*, Roscoe Arbuckle and Buster Keaton amuse early filmgoers with their kitchen antics and creative ways of eating spaghetti, while twenty years later an oversized Gus Goose in *Donald's Cousin Gus* takes the silent film stars' adventures a step farther by knitting strands of spaghetti into a sock before devouring it with evident satisfaction. Kicked out the front door, Gus makes his way back into Donald's house by way of the fridge!

Eating often means sitting down at the table and letting yourself go, as Ichabod Crane teaches us in *The Adventures of Ichabod and Mr. Toad*. During a soiree at the beautiful Katrina's house, he delights in tasting all the good things to eat before going on to face the Headless Horseman. "He who eats well is very close to God," swears the chef protagonist in the film *Big Night* (1996, directed by Stanley Tucci and Campbell Scott). All we have to do is add the direct object "apples" to the phrase and it could have been spoken by Johnny Appleseed himself, star of the 1948 Disney short of the same name.

The addition or subtraction of food, the time and place in which meals are consumed, the attitude of the participants, and the conditions in which food is eaten or kept from being eaten not only determine the pace of the action but serve to create a greater sense of humanity in each character. All it takes for the Aristocats is a bowlful of Edgar's *crème de la crème* to see their future turned upside down; Chip'n' Dale's snatching nuts and pancakes from a grouchy Donald Duck is a necessary form of revenge; Robin Hood prepares a soup as a pretext for dwelling on his chronic lovesick condition; and fatherly Baloo shows Mowgli how to gather fruits in the jungle, an important lesson in life to be sure.

Within the context of cinema as a *re-elaboration* of reality, Disney artists have paid close attention to food. It is depicted as a basic need (the classic example is *Mickey and the Beanstalk*); culinary traditions become "gastronomic deposits" (note, for instance, the use of roast turkeys and apple pies, emblems of a food culture that have been a part of Disney's earliest productions in the 1920s). Food consumption becomes a lesson in taste, though eating and drinking are more often than not a social event, an occasion for meeting others and making important exchanges (for example, the feast attended by Sir Ector, Sir Kay, and Sir Pelinore in *The Sword in the Stone*).

To be sure, to love cooking implies a reverence for imagination, fantasy, creativity. There's something magical about preparing certain recipes. This is demonstrated, literally, by Fauna in *Sleeping Beauty*. Seeing as legend steals from language, why not steal from legend its foundations in reality? Peter Pan knows the secret: "Just a little bit of pixie dust!"

Marcello Garofalo

"*isney Recipes: from Animation to Inspiration"* is a collection of enticing and imaginative recipes inspired by Disney short movies and films, from the beloved Silly Symphonies and early cartoons starring Mickey, Minnie, Donald Duck, and Goofy to favorite feature-length productions and masterpieces of today's computer animation.

From the heroism of ancient Greece to imaginary future worlds, from Europe to the United States, from South America to the Far East, there's practically no historical period or geographical area (including even previously unknown planets tucked in the farthest, most obscure reaches of the universe) that is not in some way represented in the Disney filmography. The international and multicultural flavor of this book is a reflection of such a far-reaching ideal. Tastes and traditions from around the world provide the raw materials for free-wheeling superchef

HOW TO MAKE IT

➡ Bring stock to a boil; meanwhile, mix cornstarch with a little water until smooth. Pour mixture into boiling stock, stirring well until it returns to a boil and thickens slightly.

➡ Slowly add egg whites, while stirring constantly to make "threads," as in egg drop soup.

➡ Add whole herbs and lemongrass; then remove from heat. Cool a bit before serving.

4 Servings
30 Preparation Time (minutes)

INGREDIENTS

4 cups	chicken stock
3 tbs.	cornstarch
3	egg whites, beaten slightly
1 tb.	chervil, leaves only, whole
2 tbs.	Italian parsley, leaves only, whole
1 tsp.	thyme, leaves only, whole
2 tbs.	thinly sliced chives
2 tsps.	lemongrass, purple inner part only

NUTRITION INFORMATION

Each Serving Contains	
Calories	34
Total fat	0.2 g
Saturated fat	0 g
Sodium	45 mg
Carbohydrates	5 g
Fiber	1 g
Protein	2 g

VARIATIONS

This can be easily transformed into a vegetarian dish by simply substituting vegetable broth for the chicken stock. You may also add steamed, finely diced carrots and onions and a few peas for color, texture, and flavor.

MENU IDEAS

This dish is a light, elegant beginning for a more formal meal, perhaps prefaced by "Basil's Smoked Salmon Tartar" and followed by "Sir Ector's Whiskey-Glazed Ham." For dessert, try "The Mad Hatter and March Hare's Cheesecake".

WHAT CHILDREN CAN DO

Kids may pluck parsley, chervil, and thyme leaves, from their stems which is a lot more help than the old Bruno would be any day.

Ira L. Meyer as he leads readers on a culinary expedition that spans the globe, bolstered by the firm conviction that fantasy and creativity extend well beyond national borders.

Packed with delicious, easy-to-prepare dishes, *Disney Recipes: from Animation to Inspiration* is a snap to use. The exhaustive range of selections offered—appetizers, soups, salads, pastas, main courses and side dishes, vegetarian delights, drinks, sandwiches, and desserts—is enhanced by clear, user-friendly instructions. You'll also find a wealth of useful tips and information, including nutrition analyses for each recipe, hints on where to find exotic ingredients used (and how to substitute for them in case of unavailability), menu combinations, and serving suggestions.

Ira L. Meyer provides amusing and informative introductions to each recipe, reflections that reveal the link between his scrumptious dishes and the world of Disney. Cartoon stills and rare archive sketches liven up the atmosphere, along with specially selected quotes from the pantheon of Disney characters. Photographs of the more elaborate dishes accompany recipes where a little more work is required, to further guide you along in the preparation of your Disney-inspired delights.

And since these are recipes that draw inspiration from children's stories, particular attention has been given to enlisting the aid of the kids in your kitchen. Besides the succulent sweets Ira L. Meyer has included— sure to be a hit among the young and the young at heart—there are also special sections offering suggestions on how junior chefs can lend a hand in the preparation of most dishes. Thus, cooking becomes a family activity, a way to spend quality time with the little ones while whipping up tasty and wholesome gastronomic wonders.

This unique cookbook is dedicated to Disney fans the world over, who will surely delight in exploring new food horizons alongside their favorite Disney pals. Of course, such a magnificent, fun-packed journey wouldn't be complete without a cherry on top: the book also includes two of Walt Disney's own original recipes—yes, he was an artist in the kitchen, too!

Bon appétit!

Appetizers and Condiments

Ariel's

from The Little Mermaid

"UNDER THE SEA" TEMPURA

nly Ariel—a courageous teenager who knows what she wants, is always on the lookout for new discoveries, and is ever curious as to what the world has to offer—could come up with such a dish. This easy-to-prepare recipe combines delicate tastes from land and sea, and may be used to get on a grouchy parent's good side or win over a handsome prince—or princess. For the right atmosphere, pop on Under the Sea by Sebastian the crab, and remember his advice about enjoying a life "full of bubbles."

❝IT'S, UH, NOT OFTEN THAT WE HAVE SUCH A LOVELY DINNER GUEST, EH, ERIC?❞

HOW TO MAKE IT

4	Servings
1½	Preparation Time (hours)

INGREDIENTS

1 cup	sparkling water
2	egg yolks
½ tsp.	sesame seeds*
¼ tsp.	salt
5 oz.	flour
1 cup	olive oil
½ cup	sesame oil*
½ small package	nori seaweed*
¼ cup	dry sake
½ cup	mirin*
½ cup	soy sauce
1	lime
1 small	daikon radish*

*These items are available at Asian markets and large supermarkets.

NUTRITION INFORMATION

Each Serving Contains

Calories	410
Total fat	23 g
Saturated fat	3 g
Sodium	642 mg
Carbohydrates	41 g
Fiber	2 g
Protein	6 g

➡ Pour sparkling water into a bowl. Adding egg yolks, sesame seeds, and salt to taste.

➡ Then, add flour, mixing vigorously and briefly—small lumps are okay. If batter is mixed too much, gluten will begin to develop, allowing it to absorb oil while cooking, and resulting in a tough tempura coating. Batter should have the appearance and thickness of heavy cream.

➡ Keep tempura batter cold over a bowl of ice at all times. Heat the oils to 340°-350°F.

➡ Dip seaweed into batter, coating each piece lightly and quickly, and removing any excess along the side of the bowl. Then place carefully in hot oil. Turn once quickly to sear batter. Tempura is done when lightly colored and tiny bubbles appear around edges, like those of champagne.

➡ Remove pieces from oil and place on a paper towel–lined tray, continuing until all are done. Serve immediately to prevent them from getting soggy.

TEMPURA SAUCE

➡ Combine sake, mirin, and soy sauce, warming gently in a saucepan. Serve warm, but not hot.

➡ Garnish: cut lime into wedges. Peel and grate daikon radish. Place sauce in shallow bowls, 1 bowl of sauce per person. On a dinner plate, place a small pile of the grated daikon and a wedge of lime near the edge, and the tempura in the middle.

WHAT CHILDREN CAN DO
Kids can mix dipping sauce.

Baloo's
JUNGLE AMBROSIA SALAD

*I*f we only learned to take things a bit more relaxed or "as they come," as Baloo puts it, we would all lead better, more enjoyable lives—accepting the moment for what it is, no more, no less. This is similar to the way Baloo accepts the tropical fruits that land on his big, outstretched paw. Sharing a meal with a friend and enjoying each other's company is something he would recommend. With his almost fatherly advice, Baloo is the gentle mentor most of us yearn for. This recipe includes all our bear friend's favorite fruits of the jungle—except, of course, ants. Why not replace them with poppy seeds and a bit of ginger? Such ingredients will provide that nice tickle on your tongue that Baloo's always talking about, and are surely more in line with this vegetarian dish.

**❝ DON'T SPEND YOUR TIME LOOKIN' AROUND . . .
FOR SOMETHING YOU WANT THAT CAN'T BE FOUND.
BEAUTIFUL! THAT'S REAL JUNGLE HARMONY! ❞**

HOW TO MAKE IT

4 Servings

30 Preparation Time (minutes)

INGREDIENTS

1	coconut, peeled
1	papaya, peeled, seeded
1	grapefruit, peeled, sectioned
1	prickly pear, peeled
1/2	pineapple, peeled
2	bananas, peeled
3 tbs.	poppy seeds
4 tbs.	finely diced candied gingerroot
1/4 cup	honey, warmed

➡ Preheat oven to 350°F. Peel and shave coconut with a potato peeler. Place shavings on cookie sheet and toast in oven until lightly browned (about 10 minutes). Remove and let cool.

➡ Seed the peeled papaya, then cut from top to bottom into thick slices. Arrange the slices on a large platter in a very open fan pattern. Alternate grapefruit sections with pieces of papaya.

➡ Slice peeled prickly pear into long spikes and place on top of papayas. Halve, core, and large-dice pineapple, placing chunks along bottom edge of plate.

➡ Slice bananas and intersperse them between pineapple chunks. Place poppy seeds in a bowl and add diced ginger, tossing lightly to coat. Now sprinkle these "ants" over all, then drizzle with warmed honey. Sprinkle generously with toasted coconut and serve.

NUTRITION INFORMATION

Each Serving Contains

Calories	270
Total fat	4 g
Saturated fat	3 g
Sodium	7 mg
Carbohydrates	52 g
Fiber	6 g
Protein	2 g

NOTES

Other tropical fruits may be used, such as mangoes, breadfruit, melons, red bananas.

SERVING SUGGESTIONS

Alternatively, fruit may be cut into chunks and tossed together in a salad.

WHAT CHILDREN CAN DO

Kids can arrange the fruit in patterns on the platter, learning to count as they help. Most fun of all, children can learn to make the edible ants used as garnish.

Lumiere's APPETIZERS

from Beauty and the Beast

elcoming her to a sumptuously set table, charming Lumiere attends to Belle's every need—as every good host or hostess should when friends come to dinner.

While most people don't have French butlers who double as candelabra, entertaining well is still within reach. The role of tableware is an important one, even if it doesn't actually sing and dance. For an unforgettable feast, use different dishes, platters, plates, and cups to hold your appetizers and sauces. Place them at different heights on the same table, using books covered with colored cloth as stands. You may also want to scatter flowers here and there instead of displaying them in vases. Put on some upbeat music, light lots of candles and . . . enjoy yourself!

> **RIGHT THIS WAY, MADEMOISELLE . . . BUT WHAT IS DINNER WITHOUT A LITTLE MUSIC? AND NOW WE INVITE YOU TO RELAX. LET US PULL UP A CHAIR AS THE DINING ROOM PROUDLY PRESENTS . . . YOUR DINNER!**

HOW TO MAKE IT

INGREDIENTS

Assorted crackers
Cooked ham
Pimiento-stuffed olives
Dijon mustard

Assorted crackers
Fresh cream
Caviar (black beluga variety, if you want to indulge)
Hard-boiled egg, shelled

Assorted crackers
Chicken breast, cooked
Green goddess dressing
Shredded carrot

Puff pastry sheets
Cocktail sausages
Beaten egg
Dijon mustard

Assorted crackers
Unsalted butter
Dill
Smoked salmon

French baguette slices
Country pâté
Dijon mustard
Pickles

➡ Place a small piece of cooked ham on crackers; garnish with a pimiento-stuffed olive and a dab of Dijon mustard.

➡ Combine 1 part fresh cream with 1 part black caviar and spread on crackers; top with chopped hard-boiled egg, if desired.

➡ Chop chicken into fine pieces, then mix with green goddess salad dressing; spread on crackers, garnish with shredded carrot.

➡ Wrap precooked 1-inch sausage lengths in small sections of puff pastry, then brush lightly with beaten egg. Place in a preheated 350°F oven until pastry puffs and browns, about 10 minutes. Serve warm, with Dijon mustard.

➡ Mix butter with dill and spread on crackers, then place a small piece of smoked salmon artistically on top; garnish with a sprig of dill.

➡ Spread Dijon mustard on slices of French bread, then apply pâté; garnish with a pickle.

VARIATIONS

Most anything can be cut small enough and placed on either a cracker or a leaf of lettuce or a crust of bread to be served as cocktail food. Be inventive and try to combine ingredients from some of your favorite dishes—pesto, for example, which contains basil, Parmesan cheese, garlic, olive oil, walnuts, and pinenuts. Top a toasted slice of bread with a basil leaf, a bit of shaved Parmesan cheese, and a toasted walnut—and *voilà*, you've created a canapé.

WHAT CHILDREN CAN DO

Kids can help spread sauces and decorate with garnishes.

Si and Am's
from Lady and the Tramp

APPETIZERS

his recipe is dedicated to Aunt Sarah's "angels," the two mischievous Siamese cats Si and Am, who terrorize Lady in Lady and the Tramp. *Their personalities, so similar yet different, their feline dynamism, and oriental allure have inspired this double recipe and the taste explosions it serves up, typical of Thai cooking. Sweet-and-sour "canary" wings marinated in lime juice and fish sauce for Si, goldfish "balls" for Am. But watch out—both can sabotage your diets in ways that are cunning, seductive, and full of surprises.*

One more word of advice: do not imitate Si and Am when preparing these splendid appetizers, because Aunt Sarah probably won't come running to the rescue.

**" MY DARLINGS!
MY PRECIOUS PETS! "**

HOW TO MAKE "CANARY WINGS"

4 Servings

2½ Preparation Time (hours)

INGREDIENTS

2 lb.	chicken wings
½ cup	nam pla* (fish sauce)
1 cup	lime juice
¾ cup	brown sugar
2 tbs.	sesame seeds*
2 tbs.	chili oil
2	scallions

*These items are available at Asian markets and large supermarkets.

➡ Separate wings from mini drumsticks if still attached, and marinate in a bowl with fish sauce, lime juice, and brown sugar (4 ounces) for 1 to 2 hours.

➡ Prepare brown sugar garnish in a separate bowl, combining the remaining brown sugar, sesame seeds, and chili oil, and set aside at room temperature.

➡ Thinly slice scallions and set aside at room temperature for second garnish.

➡ Preheat oven to 350°F. Line a baking pan with parchment paper for easy cleanup. Drain wings and place on pan. Bake for 20 minutes.

➡ Remove and sprinkle with brown sugar mixture, then place back in oven for an additional 5 minutes.

➡ Remove and cool for 8 minutes. Serve wings on a platter, garnished with scallions.

NUTRITION INFORMATION

Each Serving Contains

Calories	599
Total fat	33 g
Saturated fat	8 g
Sodium	111 mg
Carbohydrates	54 g
Fiber	1 g
Protein	24 g

NOTES

If you can't find nam pla, substitute a mixture of 2 tablespoons lemon juice, 2 teaspoons Worcestershire sauce, 2 tablespoons water, and ½ teaspoon brown sugar.

WHAT CHILDREN CAN DO

Kids can place wings on the baking pan and mix sugar, sesame seeds, and sugar garnish. They can also roll fish balls in egg whites and bread crumbs while counting each ball as production proceeds.

HOW TO MAKE "GOLDFISH BALLS"

SERVING SUGGESTIONS

"Canary wings" and "goldfish balls" are best served not very hot, followed by an Asian-inspired meal, perhaps "Mulan's Mahogany Chicken" with stir-fried vegetables and brown rice.

MENU IDEAS

These plates would be great as part of a football-game finger-food buffet with taste and style—not your boring old chips and dips.

➡ Dice fish into $1/4$-inch cubes (do not grind or place in food processor, as this will result in too fine a texture), then combine with ginger, lemongrass, 1 egg white, water chestnuts, salt, pepper, and sesame oil. Roll mixture into about 12 balls.

➡ Heat olive oil in a small saucepan to a frying temperature of 350°F. Dip balls in 2 beaten egg whites, then roll in bread crumbs, coating well.

➡ Place on a plate, and let dry a minute or two. Fry in batches until golden brown. While frying, combine soy sauce, lime juice, and mirin, and set aside at room temperature.

➡ When balls are golden brown, after 3 to 4 minutes, remove and place on a towel-lined plate to cool and absorb excess oils.

➡ Serve with a small bowl of dipping sauce in the middle of a plate, surrounded by the balls.

| 4 | Servings |
| 1 | Preparation Time (hours) |

INGREDIENTS

$1/2$ lb.	cod fillets
2 tsps.	grated gingerroot
1 tb.	finely chopped lemongrass (optional)
3	egg white, lightly beaten
$1/4$ cup	finely diced water chestnuts
$1/4$ tsp.	salt
1 pinch	white pepper
1 cup	olive oil
1 tsp.	roasted sesame oil*
$1/2$ cup	bread crumbs, fresh and white
$1/2$ cup	soy sauce
$1/2$ cup	lime juice
$1/2$ cup	mirin*

*These items are available at Asian markets. For mirin, see notes page 21.

NUTRITION INFORMATION

Each Serving Contains

Calories	702
Total fat	58 g
Saturated Fat	5 g
Sodium	1,016 mg
Carbohydrates	30 g
Fiber	2 g
Protein	18 g

Basil's
SMOKED SALMON TARTARE

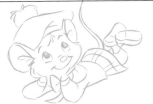

1 Servings

45 Preparation Time (minutes)

INGREDIENTS

4 oz.	smoked salmon, cold-smoked variety
1 tbs.	finely diced red onion
1/2 tsp.	finely chopped dill
1 tsp.	olive oil
1/4 tsp.	black pepper
1	hard-boiled egg, peeled
1 tsp.	capers, rinsed
6	crumpets, well toasted
3 oz.	cream cheese

inely chop smoked salmon and place in a bowl. Add red onion, dill, oil, and pepper, and toss lightly to mix.

➡ Separate egg yolk from white and chop each finely, keeping both separate. Chop capers and set aside.

➡ Mold tartare mixture in a small plastic wrap-lined bowl, then remove onto a serving platter and peel off the plastic wrap. Garnish attractively with chopped egg yolk, egg white, and capers. Lightly spread toasted crumpets with cream cheese, and place them around the tartare.

NUTRITION INFORMATION

Each Serving Contains

Calories	410
Total fat	12 g
Saturated fat	6 g
Sodium	1,456 mg
Carbohydrates	59 g
Fiber	3 g
Protein	17 g

NOTES
Smoked salmon tartare may also be spread on crackers for party canapés, then sprinkled with the same garnishes. If you can't find crumpets, buy thin English muffins and proceed accordingly.

SERVING SUGGESTIONS
Serve a mild tea for a lovely accompaniment to this treat.

❝ I BELIEVE I SMELL YOUR DELICIOUS CHEESE TARTS. WHY DON'T YOU OFFER SOME TO OUR GUESTS? ❞

The Big Bad Wolf's Dream: *from* Three Little Wolves
BARBECUED SPARERIBS WITH BLACKBERRY SAUCE

he Big Bad Wolf reminds his cubs in the Silly Symphony entitled Three Little Wolves (1936): "No one eats till Pop comes home!" He certainly can't be referring to these tasty spareribs, since our friend will never get his paws on a succulent little pig. But how would he like his ribs cooked if he did happen to come home with a fine pork booty? Tender on the inside and crunchy on the outside, in a sweet-and-sour sauce that's paw-lickin' good.

> **ROASTED PORK, GLASS OF SCHNAPPS, HAM AND EGGS, PORK 'N' CHOPS, PIGS 'N' FEET, SAUSAGE MEAT— LITTLE PIGS IS GOOD TO EAT.** "

HOW TO MAKE IT

4 Servings

1½ Preparation Time (days)

INGREDIENTS

½ tsp.	salt
¼ tsp.	black pepper
¼ tsp.	cayenne pepper
2 lbs.	spareribs
½ cup	red wine vinegar
1½ oz.	grated gingerroot
7 oz.	ketchup
¼ cup	Worcestershire sauce
½ cup	finely chopped onions
4 oz.	brown sugar
1	orange, juice only
3 oz.	coarse mustard
1 lb.	blackberries
¼ tsp.	salt
2	bay leaves
2 cups	cider vinegar

➡ Combine salt, pepper, and cayenne pepper, rub mixture over ribs, and cover. Marinate overnight in refrigerator.

➡ Combine all remaining ingredients except the cider vinegar, and place in a stockpot. After bringing to a boil, reduce to a simmer and cook for about 1 hour. Purée and strain well. Adjust salt and vinegar to taste.

➡ Preheat oven to 400°F. Place ribs in an ovenproof pan and pour the cider vinegar over them.

➡ Roast for approximately 1½ hours, until the vinegar has evaporated, turning ribs about every 20 minutes.

➡ Remove ribs from oven and lower oven temperature to 325°F.

➡ Baste ribs on both sides with sauce and bake for 15 minutes. Baste two more times at 15-minute intervals, baking for a total of 45 minutes. Slice each rib between bone and meat, and serve with sauce on the side.

NUTRITION INFORMATION

Each Serving Contains

Calories	699
Total fat	36 g
Saturated fat	13 g
Sodium	1,620 mg
Carbohydrates	77 g
Fiber	8 g
Protein	28 g

NOTES
Frozen blackberries work fine in this recipe. They may be replaced with raspberries, lingonberries, or marionberries.

VARIATIONS
As the Big Bad Wolf is the master of disguise, you, too, can be a master of disguise with this sauce. Use it on chicken, beef ribs, or even on and in burgers, turning ordinary meals into enticing gourmet dishes.

SERVING SUGGESTIONS
Potato-egg salad, and lots and lots of napkins

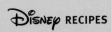

Mushu's

from Mulan

EGG ROLLS AND JUK

ushu, that charming little red dragon, who, despite his wacky ways, manages to help Mulan save the Chinese Empire, orders these special egg rolls to celebrate their accomplishments. Crunchy vegetables and quickly cooked meat and seafood are stuffed inside crispy rolls, providing necessary sustenance for battles mental and physical. They're perfect alongside a bowl of juk—rice porridge garnished with tasty little delicacies—just like Mushu prepares for Mulan, and a boost of energy for her combat training. "Look," he says, "you get porridge, and it's happy to see you." One taste of this recipe and you'll know it's true!

" CALL OUT FOR EGG ROLLS! "

HOW TO MAKE IT

4 Servings

5 Preparation Time (hours)

INGREDIENTS

$^1/_2$ package   egg roll skins* (30 pieces)

MARINADE
$^1/_2$ lb.   ground pork
$1^1/_2$ tsps.   soy sauce
1 tbs.   sake or mirin*
$^1/_2$ tsp.   toasted sesame oil
$^3/_4$ tsp.   cornstarch

FILLING
6   dried shiitake mushrooms*
4 oz.   shrimp, peeled, deveined
2 tsps.   grated gingerroot
$1^1/_2$ tsps.   sake
$^1/_2$ tsp.   cornstarch
5 tbs.   olive oil
$1^1/_2$ tsps.   minced garlic
4 oz.   cabbage, shredded
1 bunch   scallions, trimmed
4 oz.   bean sprouts, washed and dried

SAUCE
1 tb.   soy sauce
1 tb.   sake
$1^1/_2$ tsp.   toasted sesame oil*
1 dash   white pepper
$^1/_4$ tsp.   cornstarch

"GLUE" FOR ASSEMBLY
2 tbs.   water
$1^1/_2$ tsps.   cornstarch

FOR FRYING
2 cups   olive oil

* These items are available at Asian markets or large supermarkets. For mirin, see note page 21.

➡ Marinate ground pork in the marinade ingredients for 20 minutes at room temperature.

➡ Soak mushrooms in hot water until soft, remove stems, and julienne caps. Coarsely chop shrimp, then lightly mix with 1 teaspoon minced ginger, the sake, and cornstarch.

➡ Heat a nonstick sauté pan over high until very hot. Add 1 tablespoon of olive oil; when it begins to smoke, stir-fry drained pork until meat loses its pink color. Remove and drain well.

➡ Wipe pan clean, then reheat. Add 2 tablespoons olive oil; when it begins to smoke, stir-fry shrimp until opaque (2 to 4 minutes). Remove with a slotted spoon and wipe pan clean.

➡ Reheat pan, add remaining oil, and when smoking, add remaining minced ginger, the garlic, and mushrooms. Stir-fry until fragrant, about 1 to 2 minutes. Add cabbage and toss lightly over high heat until slightly limp, about $1^1/_2$ minutes. Add scallions and bean sprouts; toss lightly for 30 seconds.

➡ Quickly combine sauce mixture in a small bowl and pour it into the pan. Cook until thickened. Transfer to a colander.

SERVING SUGGESTIONS
Best served on a bed of thinly shredded cabbage with 2 sauces: the first, a hot English mustard; the second, a peach preserve thinned down with a bit of chicken stock.

MENU IDEAS
This is a great appetizer before serving "Mulan's Mahogany Chicken" for a theme meal.

VARIATIONS
Other garnishes may be used, such as julienned ham, carrots, or pickled Chinese cabbage.

WHAT CHILDREN CAN DO
Kids can help roll up the egg rolls and prepare garnishes.

HOW TO MAKE IT

➡ Drain well, and let cool, then add cooked ground pork mixture as well as the cooked shrimp mixture.

➡ Separate egg roll skins and cover with a damp cotton dish towel to keep them from drying out. In a small bowl, mix water-and-cornstarch "glue" until smooth.

➡ Arrange an egg roll skin so that pointy end is facing you. Squeeze a heaping tablespoon of filling to remove excess liquid and place toward the lower third of the skin. Roll in a cylindrical shape, folding in the two sides as you roll. Spread "glue" mixture on top edge and press to seal seam. Fry in oil at 375°F until golden brown.

JUK

➡ Bring chicken stock to a boil, then add white rice. Simmer for 1 to 2 hours, stirring occasionally so it does not stick to pot. By then, the juk should be reduced to a nice porridge consistency.

➡ Cook bacon in a nonstick sauté pan until done and remove.

➡ In the hot bacon grease, quickly fry small eggs to garnish.

➡ Divide among 4 serving bowls, garnishing each with 2 fried eggs and a strip of bacon resembling a smiley face. Serve immediately.

INGREDIENTS

JUK

1 quart	chicken stock
2 oz.	rice
4 strips	bacon
8	small eggs
2	scallions, thinly sliced

NUTRITION INFORMATION
Each Serving Contains

Calories	290
Total fat	14 g
Saturated fat	4 g
Sodium	1,366 mg
Carbohydrates	22 g
Fiber	1 g
Protein	16 g

Philoctetes'

ONION MARMALADE WITH RAISINS

4 Servings

1 Preparation Time (hours)

INGREDIENTS

2 tbs.	olive oil
1$\frac{1}{2}$ lb.	onions, peeled, thinly sliced
$\frac{1}{4}$ cup	honey
3 oz.	sherry vinegar
$\frac{1}{8}$ tsp.	salt
1 oz.	golden raisins

NUTRITION INFORMATION

Each Serving Contains

Calories	195
Total fat	10 g
Saturated fat	1 g
Sodium	700 mg
Carbohydrates	27 g
Fiber	3 g
Protein	2 g

eat oil in a nonstick pan, then add sliced onions and sauté slowly until their volume is reduced by more than half and they have attained a dark color.

➡ Add honey to onions, bring to a boil, and cook for 3 to 4 minutes on high. Add sherry vinegar, boil again, and continue cooking on high for an additional 3 to 4 minutes.

➡ Mix in raisins and salt to taste, then remove from heat.

NOTE
This relish may be stored in the refrigerator for several weeks, so you can prepare it in advance for quick holiday canapés made with store-bought pâté.

VARIATIONS
Use shallots instead of onions and currants in place of raisins, and serve on *crostini* with a bit of liver pâté.

MENU IDEAS
Simple grilled pork chops are wonderful to help show off this simple and elegant sauce. "The Three Little Pigs' Potato Pancakes with Applesauce" would be a perfect side dish.

❝ **NOW REMEMBER, KID. FIRST, ANALYZE THE SITUATION. DON'T JUST BARREL IN THERE WITHOUT THINKING. EH?** ❞

NOTES

If you can't find golden raspberries, red ones will do—but they won't match the golden luster of Briar Rose's hair.

VARIATIONS

Replace either golden or red raspberries with the juice of 2 oranges and the grated peel of one.

MENU IDEAS

Great on something as simple as toast, or when the mood strikes, over pancakes or waffles.

WHAT CHILDREN CAN DO

Kids can mash the berries in a bowl—but remember to buy extra, as they will probably eat two berries for each one they mash.

Princess Aurora's

from Sleeping Beauty

BERRIED HONEY BUTTER

Place room temperature butter in a bowl and mix with electric beater until soft and whipped.

➡ Add warmed honey, continuing to whip slowly until incorporated.

➡ Mash raspberries thoroughly, then add to honey-and-butter mixture, whipping well.

❝ **WE WANT YOU TO PICK SOME BERRIES! THAT'S IT—BERRIES!** ❞

4	Servings
30	Preparation Time (minutes)

INGREDIENTS

8 tbs.	unsalted butter, room temperature
1/4 cup	honey, warmed
2 oz.	golden raspberries

NUTRITION INFORMATION

Each Serving Contains

Calories	243
Total fat	23 g
Saturated fat	14 g
Sodium	235 mg
Carbohydrates	11 g
Fiber	1 g
Protein	1 g

Pastas

Clarabelle Cow's
TAGLIATELLE

from Cartoons

Dear, romantic Clarabelle . . . She's a star who certainly gets around. Remember her sultry flute solo in Band Concert *(1935)? What about her elegant pirouetting in* Orphans' Benefit *(1941)? And who can forget her inimitable warbling in* Mickey's Amateurs *(1937)? She's no slouch in the kitchen, either, considering the picnic treats she whips up for Mickey, Minnie, and the apple of her eye, Horace Horsecollar, in* Camping Out *(1934). Had she known about this tagliatelle dish, she surely could have used it to win over Horace. Like Clarabelle's own blend of style, grace, and simplicity, this recipe is both elegant and easy to prepare. And we all know that keeping things simple is the best way to stay out of trouble. Right, Clarabelle?*

" Moooooooooooooooooooo!!! "

HOW TO MAKE IT

4	Servings
30	Preparation Time (minutes)

INGREDIENTS

8 oz.	egg tagliatelle
8 oz.	spinach tagliatelle
3 oz.	extra-virgin olive oil
1 clove	garlic, chopped fine
2	shallots, chopped fine
8 oz.	cherry tomatoes, stemmed and washed
2 stems	basil
2 oz.	toasted bread crumbs
2	basil sprigs
	salt to taste

NUTRITION INFORMATION

Each Serving Contains

Calories	695
Total Fat	24 g
Saturated Fat	4 g
Sodium	116 mg
Carbohydrates	101 g
Fiber	5 g
Protein	17 g

➡ Bring a large pot of water to a boil, then salt well. Toss both pastas into the pot and cook until al dente.

➡ Meanwhile, heat 2 ounces of olive oil in a nonstick pan, and sauté garlic and shallots for 2 to 3 minutes, or until lightly browned and fragrant.

➡ Add cherry tomatoes, either whole or halved and seeded, as you prefer. Sauté for 2 to 3 minutes, heating tomatoes through until they begin to burst.

➡ Drain pasta well and add to sauce. Sauté an additional 2 to 3 minutes. Tear basil into large pieces and mix with pasta.

➡ Serve on a large platter. Garnish with remaining 1 ounce of olive oil, the toasted bread crumbs, and basil sprigs just prior to serving.

NOTES

If you don't have wonderful cherry tomatoes, use plum tomatoes instead. Chop them to cherry-tomato size and proceed from there.

SERVING SUGGESTIONS

Serve simply, on a large platter garnished with lots of freshly ground black pepper.

VARIATIONS

Any shape of spinach or egg pasta would work nicely in this dish, and it is not necessary to use both varieties.

WHAT CHILDREN CAN DO

Kids can wash and stem the cherry tomatoes, then rip the basil leaves into pieces.

Genie's FREE-FORM LASAGNA

from Aladdin

As elusive as a trail of smoke, Aladdin's Genie is also possessed of a boundless imagination. How else could he transform so quickly from an average, run-of-the-mill Genie, into a dragon, a slot machine Genie (very Vegas), a hi-dee-ho Genie (very Broadway) with a Cab Calloway style voice, and even the maitre d' of perhaps the most exclusive dining establishment of all time . . . your own imagination? With his amazing powers, Genie can also transform a dish as classic as lasagna into something more— a free-spirited delight, in which basic ingredients are informally combined into single-sized portions.

❝ LET'S SEE HERE. UH, CHICKEN À LA KING? NOPE. ALASKAN KING CRAB? OW, I HATE IT WHEN THEY DO THAT. CAESAR'S SALAD? ET TU, BRUTE? ❞

HOW TO MAKE IT

4 Servings

2¹/₂ Preparation Time (hours)

INGREDIENTS

16 oz.	dried lasagna noodles
4 oz.	cooked sweet Italian sausage
8	meatballs
¹/₄ cup	heavy cream
2¹/₂ cups	tomato sauce
¹/₂ cup	ricotta cheese
2 oz.	Parmesan cheese, grated
¹/₄ tsp.	black pepper
1 tbs.	chopped basil
2 oz.	mozzarella cheese, shredded
1 oz.	prosciutto ham, diced
3 tbs.	extra-virgin olive oil
1 tb.	chopped parsley

NUTRITION INFORMATION

Each Serving Contains

Calories	688
Total fat	41 g
Saturated fat	17 g
Carbohydrates	55 g
Sodium	1,410 mg
Fiber	2 g
Protein	27 g

➡ Preheat oven to 325°F. Bring a large pot of water to boiling, and salt to taste. Add lasagna noodles and cook only for 1 minute, just to soften. Drain under cold water to stop cooking. Then cut each lasagna strip into 3 or 4 squares.

➡ Cut cooked sweet Italian sausage into thin slices, and set aside. Crumble meatballs coarsely.

➡ Bring heavy cream to a boil, add ¹/₂ cup of tomato sauce, return to a boil, then remove from heat.

➡ Combine ricotta and Parmesan cheeses, black pepper, and basil, and set aside. Combine mozzarella with diced prosciutto, and set aside.

➡ Lightly oil 4 individual 4-inch oval or round ovenproof ramekins for lasagna. Place a bit of tomato sauce on the bottom of each one. Place one square of pasta on each, then place 2 tablespoons of tomato sauce on each sheet.

➡ Divide the ricotta mixture among each, then sprinkle with some of the crumbled meatballs. Top with a pasta sheet (layer 2); then divide creamed tomato sauce and most of the mozzarella mixture among each. Top with a sheet of pasta (layer 3), more tomato sauce, and sliced sausage.

➡ Place final layer of pasta and any remaining tomato sauce, top with any remaining meats, and finally with any remaining cheese mixture. It is okay if ingredients slide around a bit and lasagna is not perfectly square—that's why it's called free-form.

➡ Place in preheated oven for about 20 to 30 minutes, until completely heated through and bubbling.

➡ Remove from oven and cool for a few minutes before sprinkling with parsley and serving.

NOTES

Meatballs: use the recipe in "Lady and the Tramp's Spaghetti Bella Notte." If you have made these before, you might have extras in your freezer.
Different fillings can be used, such as cooked chicken, sautéed shrimp, sautéed spinach, or any kind of cheese.

SERVING SUGGESTIONS

This lasagna is best served in the dish it was cooked in.

WHAT CHILDREN CAN DO

Children can help with the assembly work from beginning to end.

Gus the Goose's

from Donald's Cousin Gus

SPAGHETTI WITH PEAS

With the technical experience of an industrious and productive grandmother, in the 1939 short movie Donald's Cousin Gus, *this silly goose is able to knit spaghetti with tomato sauce into a sock, and then consume it. Rather messy, one would say. He can also shuffle and deal slices of bread, cheese, and luncheon meats into sandwiches the way dealers in Las Vegas hand out cards—all before a befuddled Donald Duck. In honor of Gus the Goose's voracious appetite, here's a recipe for the spaghetti he loves so much. Of course, you won't have to knit yours, nor should you suck the peas off your neighbor's plate with a straw, either!*

" P.S. He don't eat much. "

HOW TO MAKE IT

4 Servings

45 Preparation Time (minutes)

INGREDIENTS

28 oz.	canned whole peeled tomatoes
¼ cup	extra-virgin olive oil
1 medium	onion, finely diced
1 tb.	chopped oregano
1 cup	vegetable stock
4 oz.	peas, frozen, defrosted
1 lb.	spaghetti
	salt and pepper to taste
	Parmesan cheese to taste

NUTRITION INFORMATION

Each Serving Contains

Calories	624
Total fat	17 g
Saturated fat	2 g
Sodium	656 mg
Carbohydrates	100 g
Fiber	7 g
Protein	19 g

➡ Crush tomatoes with your hands in a large bowl.

➡ Heat a large pot of water to boiling. Heat olive oil in a large nonstick sauté pan until hot. Sauté onion until softened but not browned.

➡ Add crushed tomatoes and oregano, bring to a boil, and reduce to medium heat, cooking until pasta water comes to a boil.

➡ Add salt to boiling water, and cook pasta until al dente.

➡ Add vegetable stock to tomato mixture and bring to a boil. Stir in peas, turn heat to low, add salt and pepper to taste.

➡ Drain pasta, reserving ½ cup of cooking water. Add pasta to tomato sauce and continue to cook 1 to 2 minutes. Add some of the reserved water if a bit dry.

➡ Serve on a large platter, garnished with grated Parmesan cheese.

VARIATIONS

Change the shape of the pasta to penne rigate and use "stringed" English peas still in their pods, cooked for just 1 to 2 minutes. Otherwise, proceed as above.

MENU IDEAS

Serve this pasta before "Captain Hook's Codfish Fillet" and a large portion of "Pumbaa and Timon's Potatoes with Caramelized Onions."

NOTES

Add leftover roast chicken or turkey to the tomato sauce to transform this vegetarian delight into a hearty dish.

WHAT CHILDREN CAN DO

If you are lucky enough to get fresh peas, little hands can help with the shelling. They can also crush the canned tomatoes.

Lady and the Tramp's
SPAGHETTI BELLA NOTTE

"**T**wo spaghetti especialle—*heavy on the meat-sa balls*," announces Tony in his lovable Italian accent, as he serves up this scrumptious feast to Lady and the Tramp. Amazing how each single strand of spaghetti soaks up the rich, hearty flavor of the meat combined with the refined simplicity of tasty tomato sauce. It's the ideal dish to serve your love-struck lady. There's nothing more romantic than a candlelight dinner and whispering sweet rhymes into your heartthrob's ear.

" NOW, TELL ME, WHAT'S YOUR PLEASURE? A LA CARTE? DINNER? AHA! OKAY. HEY, JOE, BUTCH-A, HE SAYS HE WANTS-A TWO SPAGHETTI ESPECIALLE HEAVY ON THE MEAT-SA-BALLS! "

HOW TO MAKE IT

6 Servings

2 Preparation Time (hours)

INGREDIENTS

1/4 cup	fresh bread crumbs
1/4 cup	milk
6 oz.	ground beef, extra lean
2 oz.	ground pork
2 oz.	ground veal
1	egg
2 tbs.	chopped parsley
1 oz.	Parmesan cheese, grated
1 1/2 tsps.	olive oil
1 1/2 cloves	garlic, chopped
1/2	medium-size onion, chopped
	salt to taste
1 dash	pepper
	tomato sauce*
1 lb.	spaghetti
	grated Parmesan cheese to taste

* See page 46

NUTRITION INFORMATION

Each Serving Contains

Calories	484
Total fat	13 g
Saturated fat	5 g
Sodium	389 mg
Carbohydrates	66 g
Fiber	3 g
Protein	24 g

➡ Preheat oven to 350°F. Soak bread crumbs in milk for a few minutes, then drain off excess milk.

➡ Mix ground beef, pork, and veal thoroughly with drained bread crumbs.

➡ Add the egg, parsley, Parmesan cheese, olive oil, garlic, and chopped onion, salt, and pepper. Taste for seasoning by frying a small amount in a nonstick pan. If taste is correct for you, shape mix into balls about 1 inch in diameter (approximately 20 meatballs in all).

➡ Arrange them on a baking sheet, making sure meatballs are not touching one another. Place in preheated oven for about 20 minutes, or until browned on the outside. Alternatively, you may fry meatballs in olive oil until browned.

➡ Heat the tomato sauce and add meatballs gently. Cover and simmer for about 25 to 30 additional minutes. When ready to serve, cook spaghetti in salted boiling water until al dente, then drain.

➡ Immediately combine spaghetti with most of the sauce and cook for an additional 3 to 4 minutes.

➡ Place spaghetti on a platter and serve meatballs alongside or on top, as seen in the film.

➡ Serve grated Parmesan in a separate bowl, for guests to add as they like. Also supply extra sauce for those who may wish to add more.

NOTES

Meatballs may be frozen with or without sauce, for later use.

Make extra meatballs and freeze them for a variety of quick recipes, such as "Genie's Free-Form Lasagna."

VARIATIONS

You may prepare this recipe, using ground beef only, but it will be heavier in texture and flavor.

WHAT CHILDREN CAN DO

Kids can mix bread crumbs and milk.

NOTE
Sauce may be frozen in small batches.

SERVING SUGGESTIONS
To truly appreciate this sauce, you must eat it accompanied by bread sticks. Candles and a red-checkered tablecloth are also a must. Don't forget to wear your white chef's hat, like Joe's. Top it all off with a song for your Lady or your Tramp.

HOW TO MAKE IT

TOMATO SAUCE

➡ Heat olive oil in a deep pan, and sauté garlic until fragrant and slightly browned. Crush tomatoes coarsely by hand; add crushed tomatoes and their juice to oil.

➡ Bring to a boil, then reduce to a high simmer. Cook uncovered for about 15 minutes, stirring occasionally.

➡ Add tomato paste, salt, pepper, sugar, and parsley. Adjust seasoning to taste, and continue to simmer 5 to 10 minutes.

➡ Add chopped basil and remove from heat.

6	Servings
30	Preparation Time (minutes)

INGREDIENTS

1/4 cup	olive oil
4 cloves	garlic, finely chopped
56 oz.	canned whole tomatoes
2 tbs.	tomato paste
1/2 tsp.	salt (or to taste)
1/2 tsp.	pepper (or to taste)
2 tsps.	sugar (or to taste)
2 tsps.	chopped Italian parsley
10	basil leaves, chopped

Minnie Mouse's
PASTA WITH THREE CHEESES

4 Servings

30 Preparation Time (minutes)

INGREDIENTS

1 lb.	shell-shaped pasta
2 tbs.	extra-virgin olive oil
1 oz.	butter
2 oz.	Parmesan cheese, grated
2 oz.	fontina cheese, finely diced
2 oz.	mozzarella cheese, finely diced
	black pepper, freshly ground to taste

NUTRITION INFORMATION

Each Serving Contains

Calories	696
Total fat	25 g
Saturated fat	12 g
Sodium	503 mg
Carbohydrates	86 g
Fiber	3 g
Protein	27 g

Bring a large pot of water to boiling, and add salt to taste. Cook pasta to al dente. Drain and reserve ¹/₂ cup of cooking water.

➡ Add olive oil and butter to pot and place over medium heat. When butter has melted, return pasta to pot. Stir in half the reserved water and cheeses.

➡ Once cheeses begin to melt, remove from heat. Add black pepper to taste. Serve on a platter, garnished with more freshly ground black pepper.

VARIATIONS

Other cheeses may be substituted for mozzarella and fontina, but the Parmesan must remain.

SERVING SUGGESTIONS

For more flourish and impact at the table, make a production of grating extra Parmesan over the platter of the finished dish, as well as grinding black pepper to taste.

❝ MICKEY! YOO-HOO! COME HERE! I'VE SUCH A NICE SURPRISE! MICKEEEEY! ❞

Pinocchio's

FARFALLE WITH LEEKS AND SAUSAGES

In his desire to become a real boy, Pinocchio takes a varied and mysterious journey through the world with Jiminy Cricket, his faithful conscience, at his side. To take on such an important task, Pinocchio certainly needs lots of energy, and this tasty, nutritious pasta dish is sure to satisfy. In honor of his Italian origins, we have selected ingredients from his country. Of course, these include farfalle, or bow tie–shaped pasta, which recalls his large blue bow tie. Don't worry, though—you won't need the Blue Fairy's help with this recipe. All it takes is a healthy dose of devotion and love.

66 I'LL NEVER LIE AGAIN.

HONEST, I WON'T! 99

HOW TO MAKE IT

4 Servings

1 Preparation Time (hour)

INGREDIENTS

2 bunches	leeks, white part only
1 lb.	Italian sausage, sweet and hot
1/4 cup	olive oil
4 tbs.	chopped Italian parsley
2 tbs.	chopped basil
2 tbs.	chopped thyme
1 lb.	farfalle pasta
	salt and pepper to taste

NUTRITION INFORMATION

Each Serving Contains

Calories	978
Total fat	52 g
Saturated fat	15 g
Sodium	877 mg
Carbohydrates	94 g
Fiber	4 g
Protein	33 g

→ Bring a large pot of water to boiling, then salt well.

→ Slice leeks in half lengthwise, then into 1-inch-thick slices. Wash thoroughly and drain in a colander.

→ Place sausages in a nonstick pan over medium heat, and cook until well browned on the outside and done on the inside, about 15 minutes.

→ Remove from pan, slice into $1/2$-inch pieces, and set aside. Heat olive oil in same pan and sauté leeks until caramelized, about 20 minutes.

→ Add sliced sausages and any accumulated juices, parsley, basil, and thyme to leeks, and hold on low heat to keep warm.

→ Place pasta in boiling water, and cook al dente. Set aside about 1 cup of the cooking water, and drain thoroughly.

→ Return drained pasta to pot, add leek-sausage mixture and half the cooking water that has been set aside. Cook for an additional 2 to 3 minutes. Adjust pepper to taste. If slightly dry, add more cooking water.

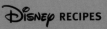

Stromboli's

PENNE WITH GRILLED VEGETABLES

Ever notice all the lovely veggies on Stromboli's table, beside his stacks of gold coins? The hot-tempered puppeteer is no doubt a lover of good food, especially when it comes to the culinary traditions of his home country, Italy. In the movie, we see him indulge in stuffed olives and sink his teeth hungrily into a raw onion. Stromboli has inspired this colorful pasta dish, loaded with grilled vegetables, garlic, onion, and fiery chili, all bathed in extra-virgin olive oil, but you won't need a cleaver to slice the ingredients of this easy-to-prepare delight.

❝ GOOD NIGHT, MY LITTLE, WOODEN GOLD MINE! ❞

HOW TO MAKE IT

4	**Servings**
1	**Preparation Time (hours)**

INGREDIENTS

8 oz.	zucchini, trimmed
1	yellow bell pepper, cored, seeded
1/2	eggplant, trimmed
1/2	red onion, peeled
4	porcini mushrooms, wiped clean
4	plum tomatoes, cut in half, seeded
3 cloves	garlic, peeled
1 tbs.	coarsely chopped thyme
3 tbs.	coarsely chopped Italian parsley
3 tbs.	coarsely chopped basil
1/2 cup	extra-virgin olive oil
1/2 tsp.	red pepper flakes
1 lb.	penne rigate
3 oz.	Romano cheese, grated
	black pepper to taste

NUTRITION INFORMATION

Each Serving Contains

Calories	844
Total fat	37 g
Saturated fat	8 g
Sodium	239 mg
Carbohydrates	106 g
Fiber	8 g
Protein	26 g

➡ Bring a large pot of water to boiling.

➡ Preheat grill or stove-top grilling pan until extremely hot. All vegetables should be sliced to the same thickness so that cooking time for each will be about the same. However, leave garlic cloves whole.

➡ Cook vegetables on hot grill until attractive grill marks appear on both sides and the slices are just limp (they will continue to cook even after removed from the grill).

➡ As the vegetables are removed from the grill, cut pieces diagonally so that they are the same size as the penne pasta; then place in a large serving bowl. Continue until all vegetables are done. Smash garlic cloves with the side of a chef's knife and add to vegetables.

➡ Add coarsely chopped herbs to vegetable mixture, along with olive oil and red pepper flakes. Meanwhile, add salt to boiling water and cook pasta al dente.

➡ Drain and mix pasta and vegetables in serving bowl. Add a bit of cooking water if too dry. Toss in half the Romano cheese and pepper, and sprinkle remaining cheese on top. Garnish with freshly ground black pepper.

VARIATIONS
Other seasonal vegetables may be substituted to your liking, but remember to keep the proportion the same: 1 pound of vegetables for every 1 pound of pasta.

SERVING SUGGESTIONS
Serve this dish with a hearty salad and crusty bread.

MENU IDEAS
Serve a bowl of "Treasure Planet's Astral Soup" before a plate of this pasta.

"So Dear to My Heart" PASTA

from So Dear to My Heart

One of Walt's favorite Disney movies, So Dear to My Heart, *brings to mind images of rural Kansas, where he spent his youth. Indeed, the traditional American "it's-whatcha-do-with-whatcha-got" inspiration behind this dish recalls a comfy, homespun atmosphere, with Granny busy at the stove and the kitchen filled with delightful smells. Watch out: with its "stick-to-it-ivity," this dish is sure to stick to your ribs and hips if you overindulge.*

66 IT'S WHAT YOU DO WITH WHAT YOU GOT THAT COUNTS! 99

HOW TO MAKE IT

6 Servings

3 Preparation Time (hours)

INGREDIENTS

1 whole (4 lbs. avg.)	roasting chicken
4 quarts (if needed)	water, or more
1	onion, diced large
1	carrot, peeled and sliced
2 ribs	celery, peeled and sliced
1 lb.	potatoes, peeled and quartered
	salt to taste
1 lb.	*casarecce* (thick double twist of rolled pasta)

NUTRITION INFORMATION

Each Serving Contains

Calories	778
Total fat	37 g
Saturated fat	10 g
Carbohydrates	58 g
Sodium	657 mg
Fiber	3 g
Protein	50 g

➡ Rinse chicken, and place in a pot with 2 quarts of water to cover. Bring to a boil and reduce to simmer, uncovered, for 1 hour.

➡ Add onion, carrot, celery, and salt; continue simmering until chicken meat is falling off bones.

➡ Bring the second 2 quarts of water to a boil; then add potatoes and salt. Cook, uncovered, until just soft.

➡ Drain potatoes well and mash coarsely. Add salt to taste as well as a bit of chicken stock, and set aside.

➡ Meanwhile, remove chicken meat from bones in large chunks. Discard skin, fat, and bones.

➡ Bring stock to a boil, add *casarecce*, and cook until done. Add chunks of chicken and serve over mashed potatoes.

SERVING SUGGESTIONS

Serve in a large soup bowl, with fresh bread and a glass of cold milk.

MENU IDEAS

A bowl of rib-sticking soup like this calls for a plate of "Cookie Carnival's Boys and Girls" for dessert.

NOTES

This soup freezes well, for those days when there just isn't enough time to cook. It may also be served without mashed potatoes.

WHAT CHILDREN CAN DO

Older kids can peel carrots and potatoes with a safety peeler.

Willie the Whale's

from Make Mine Music

PAPPARDELLE WITH SHRIMP

D o you remember that endearing character *Willie the Whale?* This adorable and talented giant of the sea could sing with three different voices simultaneously—tenor, baritone, and bass—and dreamed of becoming an opera star. Too bad Professor Tetti Tatti went out of his way to forestall Willie's aspirations. There's nothing worse than shattering someone else's dreams. To make it up to the big guy, how about a delicious plate of pasta loaded with luscious shrimp, a whale's favorite food. One bite of this harmonious taste sensation and you'll be singing, too!

" THEN WHY NOT I FIND THE OPERA SINGER IN THE BELLY OF A WHALE, HUH? "

HOW TO MAKE IT

4 Servings

45 Preparation Time (minutes)

INGREDIENTS

8 oz.	small shrimp, peeled, deveined
1 lb.	pappardelle pasta
6 tbs.	extra-virgin olive oil
2	shallots, peeled, finely diced
2 cloves	garlic, peeled, finely diced
4 oz.	plum tomatoes, seeded, diced
1 tbs.	tomato paste
12 oz.	jumbo shrimp, peeled, defrosted
10	basil leaves
	salt and pepper to taste

➡ Bring a large pot of water to boiling. Peel and devein small shrimp, and set aside. Add shells to boiling water for shrimp flavor, cook for 2 minutes, and remove shells.

➡ Salt water to taste and add pasta, stirring well.

➡ Heat extra-virgin olive oil in a sauté pan until hot, and sauté shallots and garlic 2 to 3 minutes or until fragrant, but not browned. Then add tomatoes, stirring well.

➡ Add small shrimp and continue to cook over high heat until they begin to turn pink. Add tomato paste, mixing well. Add salad shrimp and cook an additional 1 to 2 minutes, just enough to heat through. Add torn basil leaves and season with salt and pepper.

➡ By this time the pasta should be done. Set aside $^1/_2$ cup of cooking water before draining pasta. Add drained pasta to shrimp mixture, along with some of the reserved water. Toss well. Adjust seasoning if necessary; add more reserved cooking water if too dry.

➡ Garnish with freshly ground black pepper.

NUTRITION INFORMATION

Each Serving Contains

Calories	772
Total fat	25 g
Saturated fat	4 g
Sodium	289 mg
Carbohydrates	90 g
Fiber	3 g
Protein	45 g

NOTES
Can be made with only one size of shrimp as well.

SERVING SUGGESTIONS
Shredded raw spinach may be added for flavor, and to suggest the look of seaweed.

MENU IDEAS
Start off with "Tinker Bell's Golden Herb Melange," followed by a dish of "Fun and Fancy Free's Ratatouille." Finish up with some ice cream.

WHAT CHILDREN CAN DO

Kids can wash and tear basil leaves.

from Cartoons

Horace Horsecollar's
COOL PASTA
WITH "SALSA FRESCA"

MENU IDEAS
Serve with grilled vegetables for a light summer meal.

VARIATIONS
Sauté all ingredients for the salsa fresca in a nonstick pan for a few minutes, adjust salt and pepper to taste, and add HOT cooked pasta to sauce (do not rinse with cold water). Just before serving, toss in cubes of diced mozzarella for a completely new dish.

WHAT CHILDREN CAN DO
Kids can mix all ingredients together.

Bring a large pot of water to boiling, and salt well. Cook wagon-wheel pasta al dente, about 10 minutes. Drain, rinsing with cold water.

➡ In a large mixing bowl, combine remaining ingredients with half the salt and pepper.

➡ Add pasta, and let flavors absorb for a few minutes before adjusting salt and pepper.

66 WHIIIIIIINNNNNNNNYYYY!!! 99

4	Servings
40	Preparation Time (minutes)

INGREDIENTS

8 oz.	wagon-wheel pasta
4 oz.	mozzarella cheese, diced fine
1/3 lb.	plum tomatoes, seeded, coarsely chopped
1 oz.	red onions, finely diced
1 clove	garlic, finely minced
2 tbs.	chopped parsley
2 tbs.	chopped basil
1/4 cup	extra-virgin olive oil
1/2 tsp.	salt
1/2 tsp.	black pepper, coarsely ground

NUTRITION INFORMATION
Each Serving Contains

Calories	443
Total fat	22 g
Saturated fat	6 g
Carbohydrates	48 g
Sodium	401 mg
Fiber	3 g
Protein	15 g

Soups

The Black Cauldron's
FOREST SOUP

from The Black Cauldron

Many centuries ago in Prydain, a make-believe Welsh kingdom, Dallben, wise keeper of magic spells and secrets, lived in a hut deep in the forest.

In the story, he draws arcane wisdom from The Book of Three, *a mystic tome to which only he has been granted access. Dallben can be thought of as the keeper of lots of tasty soup recipes, surely prepared with the wide variety of edible mushrooms that dot the forest floor. The enticing smell of this soup bubbling away in your "cauldron" will definitely warm up a cold winter's day, and guests will be brimming with compliments as yet another culinary spell begins to take effect.*

❝ TARAN, THE POT IS BOILING OVER. TARAN! ❞

HOW TO MAKE IT

6 Servings

2 Preparation Time (hours)

INGREDIENTS

1 oz.	dried mushrooms
1/4 cup	water
2 oz.	olive oil
4 oz.	onions, finely diced
1 clove	garlic, finely minced
8 oz.	mushrooms, assorted
1	bay leaf
1/2 tsp.	thyme
8 oz.	potatoes, peeled, and 1/2-inch dice
1 tsp.	salt
1/2 package	enoki mushrooms, trimmed
	salt and pepper, to taste

➡ Soak dried mushrooms in 1/4 cup of water while you proceed with the rest of the recipe.

➡ Heat olive oil in a large soup pot, and sauté onions and garlic until soft, about 12 minutes. Meanwhile, wipe the assorted mushrooms clean and slice uniformly.

➡ Remove onions and garlic from pot and set aside. Sauté mushrooms in remaining oil until they begin to give up their liquid, about 15 minutes.

➡ After soaking dried mushrooms, squeeze out water. Coarsely chop them and add to mushroom mixture already cooking. Strain soaking water into soup pot.

➡ Add bay leaf and return onions and garlic to pot, mixing well. Add water and thyme. Bring to a boil, then simmer about 20 minutes.

➡ Add diced potatoes and salt. Continue cooking until potatoes are tender and beginning to break down, about 20 minutes.

➡ Adjust salt and pepper to taste.

➡ Garnish with enoki mushrooms and serve.

NOTES

Assorted mushrooms may include any combination of crimini, white, chanterelle, portobello, porcini, wood ear, hen of the woods, black trumpet, etc. If enoki mushrooms are not available, simply reserve a few slices of any other sautéed mushrooms to use as garnish. Vegetable, chicken, or veal stock could easily replace water for a heartier soup.

SERVING SUGGESTIONS

Serve this soup in small, hollowed-out round breads that have been left out overnight to dry. Make garlic bread with the tops that have been removed and use as a garnish.

VARIATIONS

Puree this soup; then add heavy cream and sherry for a completely different twist.

NUTRITION INFORMATION

Each Serving Contains

Calories	144
Total fat	10 g
Saturated fat	2 g
Carbohydrates	13 g
Sodium	436 mg
Fiber	2 g
Protein	3 g

Cinderella's
HERB AND EGG WHITE SOUP

from Cinderella

Soup as light and beautiful as Cinderella's wedding gown, almost gossamer-like, yet as strong as her will, this light bit of nourishment will soothe the soul and warm the belly. It could even placate Lucifer the cat or melt the chill out of Lady Tremaine when served with a warm smile. Your friends will love it, and like Cinderella's mice pals Jaq and Gus, they'll try to outdo one another in the affection they show you after they've eaten a bowlful. You can imagine that tonight they will wash the dishes and clean up for you, singing, "We want to help our Cinderelly," as they work. Oh, yes—there is no pumpkin in this dish, since there might be a fairy godmother with a magic wand in her purse among your guests.

❝ THEY CAN'T ORDER ME TO STOP DREAMING. ❞

HOW TO MAKE IT

4 Servings

30 Preparation Time (minutes)

INGREDIENTS

4 cups	chicken stock
3 tbs.	cornstarch
3	egg whites, beaten slightly
1 tb.	chervil, leaves only, whole
2 tbs.	Italian parsley, leaves only, whole
1 tsp.	thyme, leaves only, whole
2 tbs.	thinly sliced chives
2 tsps.	lemongrass, purple inner part only

NUTRITION INFORMATION

Each Serving Contains

Calories	34	
Total fat	0.2	g
Saturated fat	0	g
Sodium	45	mg
Carbohydrates	5	g
Fiber	1	g
Protein	2	g

➡ Bring stock to a boil; meanwhile, mix cornstarch with a little water until smooth. Pour mixture into boiling stock, stirring well until it returns to a boil and thickens slightly.

➡ Slowly add egg whites, while stirring constantly to make "threads," as in egg drop soup.

➡ Add whole herbs and lemongrass; then remove from heat. Cool a bit before serving.

VARIATIONS

This can be easily transformed into a vegetarian dish by simply substituting vegetable broth for the chicken stock. You may also add steamed, finely diced carrots and onions and a few peas for color, texture, and flavor.

MENU IDEAS

This dish is a light course for a more formal meal, beginning with "Basil's Smoked Salmon Tartare" and followed by "Sir Ector's Whiskey-Glazed Ham." For dessert, try "The Mad Hatter and March Hare's Cheesecake."

WHAT CHILDREN CAN DO

Kids may pluck parsley, chervil, and thyme leaves, from their stems which is a lot more help than the old Bruno would be any day.

The Grasshopper and the Ants' *from* The Grasshopper and the Ants
LENTIL SOUP

In a large soup kettle, combine all ingredients except tomatoes. Bring to a boil and simmer over low heat for 1½ hours. Add tomatoes and simmer another 20 to 30 minutes.

➡ When ready to serve, drizzle extra-virgin olive oil over each dish just before serving.

❝ SO TAKE YOUR FIDDLE . . . AND PLAY! ❞

| 4 | Servings |
| 2 | Preparation Time (hours) |

INGREDIENTS

8 oz.	dried lentils, washed, picked over
1¼ quarts	water
1	celery stalk, peeled, chopped
½	medium-size onion, chopped
1	carrot, peeled, chopped
½ tsp.	minced garlic
1 small	bay leaf
¼ tsp.	chopped fresh thyme
2 tsps.	chopped parsley
3	plum tomatoes, seeded, chopped
¼ cup	extra-virgin olive oil
	salt and pepper to taste

NUTRITION INFORMATION

Each Serving Contains

Calories	350
Total fat	15 g
Saturated fat	2 g
Carbohydrates	40 g
Sodium	107 mg
Fiber	19 g
Protein	17 g

Merlin's
MAGICAL BROTH

10 Servings

1 Preparation Time (hours)

INGREDIENTS

¹/₄ cup	olive oil
4 oz.	carrots, chopped
4 oz.	celery, chopped
2 oz.	onions, chopped
1 clove	garlic, minced
¹/₄ tsp.	turmeric
5 sprigs	parsley
2 tbs.	chopped thyme
2	bay leaves
2 oz.	yellow split peas
2 quarts	water
	salt and pepper to taste

eat oil in a stockpot. Add carrots, celery, onions, garlic, and turmeric and sauté for 10–12 minutes, or until fragrant and lightly browned. Add parsley, thyme, bay leaf, and yellow split peas, and sauté an additional 8 to 10 minutes.

➡ Add water, bring to a boil, and reduce to a simmer. Cook 15 to 20 minutes for a "brothlike" taste. Strain after seasoning with salt and pepper.

➡ If you plan to use this stock for a hearty soup, continue to simmer for an additional 15 minutes before straining; then season with salt and pepper.

➡ REMEMBER: DO NOT BOIL; OTHERWISE YOUR STOCK WILL BECOME CLOUDY.

> ❝ **YOU CALL WASHING DISHES AND SWEEPING FLOORS A WORK OF EVIL?** ❞

NUTRITION INFORMATION

Each Serving Contains

Calories	161
Total fat	7 g
Saturated fat	1 g
Carbohydrates	18 g
Sodium	176 mg
Fiber	5 g
Protein	4 g

NOTES
Turmeric is a dry spice made from the root of the tropical Asian plant of the same name. It is the color of curry powder, but much milder, and should be available in the dried-spice section of most supermarkets. As an alternative, use ¹/₈ teaspoon saffron.

Freeze unused portion of the broth in small containers for future use, so you won't have to make this stock every time a recipe calls for it.

SERVING SUGGESTIONS
Use in place of chicken stock in any recipe.

MENU IDEAS
Combined with noodles and various vegetables, this stock would be great with a grilled cheese sandwich.

Louis's

SEAFOOD CHOWDER

The word "chowder" comes from the French *chaudier*, which refers to the soup pot itself. Chowder prepared in such a pot generally contains potatoes. This is no news to a refined French chef like Louis, and considering his passion for seafood dishes, he must have served this tasty dish on many occasions to guests at Prince Eric's castle. Prepared "in the classic technique," seafood chowder is actually quite easy to make, provided you don't have to go chasing a stray crab all over your kitchen! And remember: there are no crabs in this recipe!

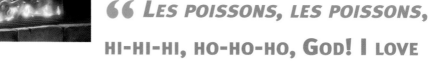

❝ *LES POISSONS, LES POISSONS,* HI-HI-HI, HO-HO-HO, GOD! I LOVE LITTLE FISHES, DON'T YOU? HERE'S SOMETHING FOR TEMPTING THE PALATE, PREPARED IN THE CLASSIC TECHNIQUE! ❞

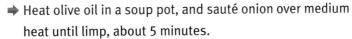

6 Servings

1 Preparation Time (hours)

INGREDIENTS

2 tbs.	olive oil
1 small	onion, finely chopped
3 tbs.	flour
2 cups	water
8 oz.	potatoes, peeled, in $\frac{1}{2}$-inch dice
8 oz.	cod fillet, in $\frac{1}{2}$-inch cubes
8 oz.	medium shrimp, peeled and deveined
24	cherrystone clams
2 cups	clam juice
2 tsps.	chopped thyme
1 cup	light cream
1 tb.	chopped parsley
	salt and pepper to taste

➡ Heat olive oil in a soup pot, and sauté onion over medium heat until limp, about 5 minutes.

➡ Add flour and cook 3 to 4 minutes; then add water and bring to a boil.

➡ Add potatoes, bring to a boil, and cook for about 5 minutes.

➡ Add cod, shrimp, and clams, and simmer, covered, 5 minutes.

➡ Add remaining ingredients and bring to a boil before removing from heat.

➡ Allow chowder to stand for 5 to 10 minutes before adjusting salt and pepper to taste.

NUTRITION INFORMATION

Each Serving Contains

Calories	310
Total fat	14 g
Saturated fat	5 g
Carbohydrates	21 g
Sodium	792 mg
Fiber	1 g
Protein	25 g

SERVING SUGGESTIONS

Serve with tiny oyster crackers; however, a simple hunk of French bread would be equally at home here.

VARIATIONS

Any firm white fish may be used in place of cod and shrimp, such as halibut, hake, tilefish, or haddock.

MENU IDEAS

This chowder is best served on a cold night, with a spinach-and-bacon salad and toasted cheese sandwiches.

Treasure Planet's

from Treasure Planet

J ASTRAL SOUP

John Silver is the cyborg chef who runs the kitchen aboard the Legacy, and it's his mission to keep crew members' bellies full as they journey to the outer reaches of space. Surely, a bowl of this astral soup will give you enough stamina to travel the galaxies and explore supernovas, black holes, and unbridled space storms, though it is also suited to more earthbound adventures. So whether you're rocketing through our world or zooming across a parallel universe, you'll need lots of good food for a clear head, bright eyes, and bodily strength in order to explore and discover what lies ahead.

" HERE . . . NOW . . . HAVE A TASTE O' ME FAMOUS BONZABEAST STEW! "

HOW TO MAKE IT

4 Servings

1 Preparation Time (hours)

INGREDIENTS

2 tbs.	extra-virgin olive oil
1 clove	garlic, finely minced
3	shallots, sliced
2 cups	water
6	Roma tomatoes, halved and seeded
1 tb.	tomato paste
1 strip	orange peel
$^1/_4$ tsp.	chopped thyme
2 pinches	saffron
1 bulb	fennel, tops reserved
4 oz.	cod fillet, cubed
12	mussels
8	clams, cherrystones
8	sea scallops with roe, in shell if possible
4	langoustine or giant shrimp, head on
4	squid, whole and cleaned
3 tbs.	chopped parsley

➡ Heat olive oil in a large Dutch oven, and sauté garlic and shallots until fragrant, 3 to 4 minutes. Add water and bring to a boil.

➡ Coarsely chop tomatoes, and add to boiling water, along with tomato paste, orange peel, thyme, and saffron. Boil for 5 minutes.

➡ Slice fennel about $^1/_2$ inch thick, chop the feathery tops, and set both aside separately.

➡ Add cod fillet to boiling liquid, reduce heat to medium, and cook, covered, 2 to 3 minutes. Add mussels, clams, scallops, and shrimp, and cook, covered, 2 to 3 minutes at medium heat.

➡ Remove tentacles from squid and split open. Rinse to clean. Slice into thick segments and add to soup, along with sliced fennel.

➡ Cover and cook an additional 1 to 2 minutes. Remove cover and scatter chopped fennel tops and chopped parsley onto surface. Serve from cooking pot to table.

NUTRITION INFORMATION

Calories	667
Total fat	20 g
Saturated fat	3 g
Carbohydrates	35 g
Sodium	1,452 mg
Fiber	3 g
Protein	85 g

NOTES

A variety of fish may be used, depending upon availability. However, there are a few exceptions: do not use sole, as it is too thin and will break down within minutes; avoid salmon, mackerel, or herring, as they are too strong in flavor.

WHAT CHILDREN CAN DO

Little hands can pluck thyme and parsley leaves and fennel tops.

Robin Hood's

from Robin Hood

CREAMY CARROT SOUP

obin Hood prepares this soup with vegetables gathered by his friends in the heart of Sherwood Forest. His expression is dreamy, and he wears a gratified smile as he slowly and ineffectually stirs the broth inside the great kettle placed over a wood fire. Of course, we can forgive Robin for taking it so easy—it must be love. Luckily, Little John and Friar Tuck, obviously possessed of huge appetites as well as a sense of practicality, are there to watch over things and make sure the soup doesn't stick to the bottom of the pot. You'll have to remember to do the same. But don't be alarmed if you happen to find yourself distracted by amorous daydreams—love and cooking were made for each other.

" HEY, LOVER BOY. HOW'S THAT GRUB COMIN', MAN? I'M STARVED . . . AH, FORGET IT. YOUR MIND'S NOT ON FOOD. "

HOW TO MAKE IT

6 Servings

1½ Preparation Time (hours)

INGREDIENTS

3 oz.	olive oil
8 oz.	onions, peeled, in ½-inch dice
1 lb.	carrots, sliced
1 quart	water
1 tb.	salt
1 bunch	sage, leaves only

NUTRITION INFORMATION

Each Serving Contains

Calories	163
Total fat	14 g
Saturated fat	2 g
Carbohydrates	9 g
Sodium	1,200 mg
Fiber	3 g
Protein	1 g

➡ Heat 2 ounces of olive oil in a soup pot, and sauté onions until coffee colored.

➡ Remove half the onions and set aside. Add carrots and water to pot, and bring to a boil. Add salt and reduce to a simmer, cooking until carrots begin to break down and soup thickens somewhat.

➡ In a small saucepan, heat the remaining olive oil until very, very hot; then add sage leaves and sauté until crisp. Remove and drain on a paper towel, saving oil.

➡ After 1 hour, soup should have the consistency of porridge. If you wish, you may help it along with a potato masher. Add caramelized onions that have been set aside, and adjust salt to taste.

➡ Divide soup among 6 bowls and garnish each with a bit of the sage-flavored olive oil and fried sage leaves.

SERVING SUGGESTIONS

Garnish with fresh ground pepper. Serve *crostini* spread with a soft goat cheese alongside.

MENU IDEAS

A bowl of this might set you hankering for "Pecos Bill's Grilled Rib-Eye Steak with Red-Eye Gravy" and a side of grilled asparagus.

WHAT CHILDREN CAN DO

Kids can pluck sage leaves from stems.

Snow White's

from Snow White and the Seven Dwarfs

WINTER VEGETABLE SOUP

imple," "easy to prepare," and "healthy" are words to describe the soup Snow White whips up for the Seven Dwarfs. Made from vegetables that could have been stored in the cold cellar of their cottage in the forest (remember, there was no electric refrigeration back then), this slow-cooked porridge has an aroma that permeates the house on a chilly day, creating a warm welcome. The expression on your face is likely to evoke Happy's when treated to a bowlful, and if there happen to be any Grumpies in the crowd, they're sure to change their tunes as well.

" AHH! SOUP! HOORAY!"

"UH, UH, UH. JUST A MINUTE. SUPPER'S NOT QUITE READY. YOU'LL JUST HAVE TIME TO WASH. "

HOW TO MAKE IT

6 Servings

1½ Preparation Time (hours)

INGREDIENTS

1 quart	water
1 lb.	carrots, peeled, coarsely chopped
8 oz.	parsnips, peeled, coarsely chopped
8 oz.	potatoes, peeled, coarsely chopped
4 oz.	onion, peeled, coarsely chopped
	salt and pepper to taste

➡ Combine all ingredients in a stockpot, bring to a boil, and reduce to a simmer, stirring now and then until the vegetables begin to break down. After about 1 hour, soup should have the consistency of porridge.

➡ Salt to taste and serve with fresh ground pepper.

NOTES
If parsnips are not available, simply replace them with more potatoes.

MENU IDEAS
Serve with small rolls, perhaps using the recipe for "Mr. Toad's Irish Soda Bread." Knead dough into small rolls instead of one large loaf.

VARIATIONS
Finish the soup with 8 ounces of heavy cream to give it a silky, rich flavor.

NUTRITION INFORMATION

Each Serving Contains

Calories	80
Total fat	0 g
Saturated fat	0 g
Sodium	281 mg
Carbohydrates	19 g
Fiber	4 g
Protein	2 g

WHAT CHILDREN CAN DO

Older kids can peel and dice carrots, parsnips, and potatoes, with a safety peeler.

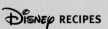

Widow Tweed's

CHEDDAR SOUP WITH HERBED CRISPS

O n a cold, blustery night, imagine a pot of this soup on Widow Tweed's stove top. The cheese in it probably came from the milk she got from Abigail, her cow. Picture her now, bending over the oven, using her apron to protect her hands from the hot pan, taking out fragrant, tasty herbed crisps—the perfect accompaniment to this lovingly made, soul-satisfying soup. From her farmhouse kitchen to yours, this recipe could be the bridge over time and troubles, helping you to shake off the "chills" of a somewhat "cold and impersonal" world. And remember to tell your "cub" that a good friend is worth his weight in gold.

> **" I WANT TO FIND OUT WHAT THAT SMELL IS. "**

HOW TO MAKE IT

4 Servings

40 Preparation Time (minutes)

INGREDIENTS

1 quart	chicken stock
4 tbs.	butter
2 tbs.	flour
1 cup	light cream
1 cup	shredded sharp cheddar cheese
$1/2$ tsp.	paprika
	salt and pepper to taste
$1/2$ sheet	puff pastry, frozen
4 tbs.	chopped parsley
1 tb.	chopped thyme
2 tbs.	chopped rosemary
$1/2$ tsp.	ground black pepper
2 tbs.	grated Parmesan cheese

NUTRITION INFORMATION

Each Serving Contains

Calories	52
Total fat	43 g
Saturated fat	22 g
Sodium	1,179 mg
Carbohydrates	22 g
Fiber	1 g
Protein	14 g

➡ Bring chicken stock to a boil over medium heat; reduce to a simmer for 10 minutes.

➡ Melt 2 tablespoons of butter in a small pan. Add flour to make a roux, and cook over medium heat, stirring for 5 to 6 minutes. It should turn a light straw color, not dark. Stir in cream until mixture is smooth and thick, with no lumps. Add to chicken stock mixture, blend well, and continue to simmer for several minutes, or until soup has thickened a bit, about the consistency of pancake batter.

➡ Slowly add cheese, stirring constantly. Add paprika, salt, and pepper to taste. Do not allow soup to boil.

➡ Thaw puff pastry to room temperature on a sheet of parchment paper. Combine 2 tablespoons of parsley, thyme, rosemary, and pepper, then spread on puff pastry. Roll pastry from the long side until you have a tight roll. Refrigerate until firm. Preheat oven to 400°F. Remove firm dough from refrigerator and cut $1/2$-inch slices. Place on parchment-lined cookie sheet. Sprinkle with Parmesan cheese and place in preheated oven for 10 to 12 minutes or until golden brown. Allow to cool. Serve alongside soup.

WHAT CHILDREN CAN DO

Little hands can help shred cheese, and roll crisps before baking.

Wise Little Hen's ROASTED CORN SOUP

from The Wise Little Hen

The Wise Little Hen stars in the well-known 1934 Silly Symphony of the same name (in which Donald Duck made his first-ever big-screen appearance). The moral of her tenacity is that hard work pays off, while all swindlers and lazybones deserve is a healthy dose of castor oil! At the end of this short movie, our unstoppable little dynamo whips up a scrumptious meal for her chicks, featuring corn soup, corn fritters, corn bread, and corn on the cob. So, directly from her table to yours, here are the secrets to her super roasted corn soup.

> **66 A LITTLE HEN — INDUSTRIOUS AND WISE AS ANY HEN CAN BE — FINDS HAPPINESS IN DAILY TASKS! AN EXCELLENT PHILOSOPHY! 99**

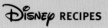

HOW TO MAKE IT

4 Servings

1½ Preparation Time (hours)

INGREDIENTS

6 ears	corn, shucked
3 cups	vegetable stock
1 medium	onion, chopped
2 medium	potatoes, peeled and diced
1 medium	tomato, seeded and chopped
1 tb.	chopped parsley
	salt and pepper to taste

NUTRITION INFORMATION

Each Serving Contains

Calories	157
Total fat	2 g
Saturated fat	0.5 g
Sodium	853 mg
Carbohydrates	35 g
Fiber	8 g
Protein	6 g

➡ Preheat broiler or grill. Cook ears of corn until nicely browned on all sides, at which point you will begin to hear them popping. Set aside to cool.

➡ Heat vegetable stock in a pot until boiling. Reduce to a simmer, add onion, and potatoes, and cook gently, uncovered, for 10 to 12 minutes.

➡ Hold roasted ears of corn in large bowl and scrape kernels off from top to bottom with the back of a knife. Place kernels and cobs in hot stock. Simmer for about 15 minutes.

➡ Add tomato and parsley. Cook for an additional 2 to 3 minutes.

➡ Add salt and pepper to taste. Before serving, carefully remove cobs, scrapping off any additional corn kernels.

NOTES
If fresh ears of corn are not available, "roast" frozen corn on a pan under the broiler until kernels brown and begin to pop.

SERVING SUGGESTIONS
Serve in a large soup bowl with large, hot buttermilk biscuits on the side.

WHAT CHILDREN CAN DO

Little hands can shuck the corn (be sure that there is no silk left on the ears).

Madam Mim's DRAGON SOUP

You're sure to win all your battles after a hefty serving of this soup, which is as magical as Madam Mim herself. She'd be only too happy to help you make a mess of your kitchen while cooking up this unpredictable potion. Follow the recipe or break the rules and use whatever is in your refrigerator — the stranger the better for the ever-changing Madam Mim. This easy-to-prepare, one-pot meal is enough to nourish and satisfy the hungry dragon in all of us.

> **❝ WHY, BOY, I'VE GOT MORE MAGIC IN ONE LITTLE FINGER . . . NOW DON'T TELL ME YOU'VE NEVER HEARD OF THE MARVELOUS MADAM MIM??? ❞**

HOW TO MAKE IT

4 Serving Size

1 Preparation Time (hours)

INGREDIENTS

1 oz.	extra-virgin olive oil
2 ribs	celery, peeled and thinly sliced
1	green bell pepper, seeded, 1/2 inch diced
1 bunch	scallions, thickly sliced
1/2 tsp.	cayenne pepper
10 small	Roma tomatoes, seeded and diced
4 oz.	Andouille sausage, thinly sliced
1/4 cup	rice
8 oz.	sliced okra
1 quart	water
2/3 tsp.	salt
1/4 tsp.	pepper
8 oz.	medium shrimp, peeled and cleaned
	hot sauce to taste

NUTRITION INFORMATION

Each Serving Contains

Calories	374
Total fat	21 g
Saturated fat	5 g
Sodium	691 mg
Carbohydrates	31 g
Fiber	6 g
Protein	19 g

➡ Heat olive oil in a stockpot, sauté celery, bell pepper, scallions, cayenne, and tomatoes, for 10 to 12 minutes, or until softened.

➡ Add sausage, cook for an additional 5 to 7 minutes.

➡ Add rice and continue to sauté for 10 to 12 minutes.

➡ Add okra, water, salt and pepper, and bring to a boil; reduce to a simmer and partially cover pot until rice is tender, about 15 minutes.

➡ Add shrimp, stir well and cover; continue to cook for 4 to 5 minutes, until shrimp turn pink.

➡ Adjust seasonings as needed and pass the hot sauce when serving.

NOTES

If you're unable to find Andouille sausage, substitute a spicy sausage of your choice.

VARIATIONS

This soup may be made with different types of broth. You may also add a quarter pound of cooked chicken, crab, duck, turkey, or beef when mixing in shrimp.

SERVING SUGGESTIONS

Best served in a large bowl with warm cornbread.

MENU IDEAS

A great fan of purple and pink, Madam Mim would serve this dish with "The Cheshire Cat's Marinated Fish Salad."

WHAT CHILDREN CAN DO

Children can wash the vegetables.

Make Mine Music's

from Make Mine Music

B DOUBLE SOUP

ring the first batch of vegetable stock to a boil; then add scallions and peas. Cook until soft, about 20 minutes. Remove solids to a blender and add mint leaves, processing until smooth. Add a little cooking liquid if needed, to make a smooth puree.

➡ Add cream to hot liquid and return to boil; then add pureed solids. Heat through; then salt to taste.

➡ In a separate pot, bring the second batch of vegetable stock to a boil; then add carrots. Cook on high until carrots are soft, about 20 minutes.

➡ Remove solids to a blender and add grated ginger, processing until smooth. Return puree to simmering stock, and add cream. Salt to taste.

➡ When ready to serve, use a large spatula to divide each soup bowl in two and, with different ladles, pour one soup at a time into each half of the bowl; then remove the spatula when both soups have been added.

6 Servings

1 Preparation Time (hours)

INGREDIENTS

PEA SOUP

2 cups	vegetable stock
2	trimmed and chopped scallions
8 oz.	fresh spring peas
1/2 bunch	mint, leaves only
1/4 cup	light cream
	salt to taste

CARROT SOUP

2 cups	vegetable stock
12 oz.	peeled and diced carrots
2 tbs.	freshly grated gingerroot
1/4 cup	light cream
	salt to taste

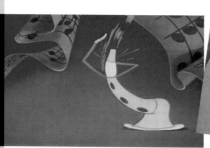

*E*ntrées

Captain Hook's

CODFISH FILLET

When Peter Pan wants to insult his archenemy Captain hook, he can think of nothing worse to call him than "Codfish!" If only Peter had known how tasty cod is, perhaps he would have called the captain something else. In any case, Peter's gibe inspired this tasty dish. The special sauce, made of roasted red peppers with a smoky aroma, was, however, inspired by the finery and colors of the captain's wardrobe, along with his impetuousness. If you're looking for kitchen helpers, make sure they steer clear of Mr. Smee's technique for shaving the captain when it comes to peeling the peppers.

" WELL, ALL RIGHT. IF YOU SAY YOU'RE A CODFISH! "

HOW TO MAKE IT

4 Servings

1¼ Preparation Time (hours)

INGREDIENTS

2	red bell peppers, stemmed, seeded
1 clove	garlic, minced
3 tbs.	extra-virgin olive oil
½ tsp.	chopped fresh thyme
	salt and pepper to taste
1½ lb.	codfish fillets, 4 pieces
2 tbs.	chopped parsley

NUTRITION INFORMATION

Each Serving Contains

Calories	325
Total fat	13 g
Saturated fat	1 g
Carbohydrates	19 g
Sodium	229 mg
Fiber	4 g
Protein	38 g

➡ Preheat broiler for 30 minutes. Wash red bell peppers, and broil until blackened completely on all sides. Remove peppers to a clean paper bag, and roll top down to close. Let cool on a plate for 30 minutes; then peel off blackened skin. It doesn't matter if pieces tear apart, since you will be pureeing them in a food processor or blender.

➡ Process roasted red peppers, garlic, and olive oil until mixture is a rough puree. Add thyme, salt, and pepper to taste. Hold at room temperature while cooking codfish, or refrigerate up to 4 days before using. If mixture is made in advance, remove from refrigerator and allow to reach room temperature before using.

➡ Broil codfish fillets to desired degree of doneness. One-inch thick steaks (measured at the thickest part) require 10 minutes, which should serve as a guideline.

➡ When fish is ready, pour part of the sauce on the serving platter; place cooked fish on top. Spoon a bit of sauce on one end of each fillet as well.

➡ Sprinkle the dishes with the parsley before serving.

Cookie's

SPECIAL CHILI

his dish is a blend of Cookie's version of the four basic food groups: beans, bacon, whiskey, and lard. It is cooked slowly, just the way he would prepare it on the back of a chuck wagon—only "gussied" up a bit with some vegetables and tomatoes. While it's chock-full of beans and cubed beef, luckily for the rest of us it's not as greasy as Cookie might like. A fit repast for any hard-working soul, it's sure to satisfy the most ravenous appetites.

❝ PUT SOME MEAT ON THEM BONES! ❞

HOW TO MAKE IT

4 Servings

3 Preparation Time (hours)

INGREDIENTS

2 strips	bacon, smokiest type
1 oz.	shortening
1 lb.	beef, top round, in $\frac{1}{2}$-inch cubes
8 oz.	onions, in $\frac{1}{2}$-inch dice
1 clove	garlic, finely minced
$\frac{1}{2}$	green bell pepper, in $\frac{1}{2}$-inch dice
$\frac{1}{2}$	red bell pepper, in $\frac{1}{2}$-inch dice
$\frac{1}{2}$ cup	rye whiskey
$\frac{1}{2}$ tsp.	chopped oregano
3 tbs.	chili powder, mild
$\frac{1}{4}$ tsp.	cayenne pepper
$\frac{1}{2}$ tsp.	ground cumin
$1\frac{1}{2}$ tsps.	salt
$\frac{1}{4}$ cup	canned tomatoes, diced, with juice
$\frac{1}{2}$ cup	water
1 lb	canned pinto beans, drained and rinsed

➡ Heat a heavy, deep pot, and sauté bacon and shortening. Remove bacon when crisp, and set aside.

➡ Add beef cubes in 4 separate batches; sear well, to a dark brown color; hold cooked meat in a bowl while cooking remaining cubes.

➡ Sauté onions and garlic until soft, then remove to a separate bowl.

➡ Sauté bell peppers until soft, then remove to bowl containing onions and garlic.

➡ Add whiskey to hot pan, carefully burning off alcohol. When flames die down, add oregano, chili powder, cayenne, cumin, salt, canned tomatoes, and water. Bring to a boil (it should be spicy and salty at this time).

➡ Crumble cooked bacon and add to liquid, along with cooked meat. Return to a boil, then reduce to a simmer. Cook, partially covered, at medium heat for about 1 hour, stirring every 15 minutes.

➡ Add sautéed vegetables and canned beans, mixing well. Continue to cook, partially covered, over low heat for about 1 hour, or until meat is tender.

➡ Chili shouldn't be dry, but somewhat soupy. If necessary, add a bit more water and taste for seasonings before serving. Dish should be fairly spicy, but not overpowering.

NUTRITION INFORMATION

Each Serving Contains

Calories	519
Total fat	21 g
Saturated fat	8 g
Carbohydrates	32 g
Sodium	1,732 mg
Fiber	9 g
Protein	35 g

NOTES
If you can't find chili powder, grind 1 large dried red chili pod with either a mortar and pestle or a clean coffee grinder. You can use 1 cup of beer instead of whiskey (reduce water accordingly).

SERVING SUGGESTIONS
Best served in a large, deep bowl.

MENU IDEAS
Serve chili with corn bread, shredded cheddar cheese, and chopped raw onions. Don't forget to have a bottle of hot sauce on hand for those who like their chili super spicy.

Esmeralda's

TURKEY PICCATA

smeralda, the gorgeous gypsy who encourages Quasimodo to abandon his reclusive ways and bask in the joy that the world has to offer, is a complex, multifaceted character. She can be sweet yet combative, proud yet unselfish, seductive yet affectionate. This dish may look plain and simple, but the capers are as feisty as her eyes, while the sauce is as smooth as her moves, and has an acerbic edge. Prepare this dish for your own Feast of Fools, or a romantic dinner for two, as Phoebus suggests: "Candlelight, privacy, music—what better place for hand-to-hand combat?" However, it should be with knives and forks, don't you think? And if you happen to have a lively pet goat, don't begrudge it a bowl of salt to lick.

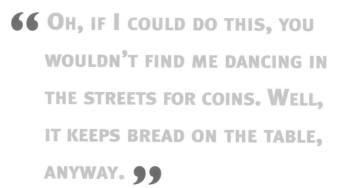

❝ OH, IF I COULD DO THIS, YOU WOULDN'T FIND ME DANCING IN THE STREETS FOR COINS. WELL, IT KEEPS BREAD ON THE TABLE, ANYWAY. ❞

HOW TO MAKE IT

4	Servings
1¼	Preparation Time (hours)

INGREDIENTS

½ cup	olive oil
2 tbs.	capers, drained and rinsed
2 tbs.	flour
¼ tsp.	salt
¼ tsp.	white pepper
½ tsp.	thyme, dried and ground
2 lb.	raw boneless turkey breast, sliced ¼-inch thick
¼ cup	white wine
2	lemons
1 oz.	butter
1 tb.	chopped parsley

NUTRITION INFORMATION

Each Serving Contains

Calories	599
Total fat	38 g
Saturated fat	9 g
Carbohydrates	10 g
Sodium	358 mg
Fiber	0 g
Protein	46 g

➡ Heat oil in a nonstick sauté pan until very hot, while drying capers on paper towels.

➡ Place capers in very hot oil; they will spatter, so use a spatter shield if you have one. As they sauté, they will brown a bit, open up, and become crispy within several minutes. Remove from oil and place on paper towels to drain completely. Turn heat of oil down to medium.

➡ Combine flour, salt, pepper, and thyme, and dust turkey slices thoroughly. Sauté for about 5 minutes in hot oil, until lightly browned on both sides. Remove to a platter and keep warm while repeating with the remaining slices.

➡ When all are done, pour off oil and return pan to heat. Deglaze pan with wine, scraping up any browned bits on the bottom. When wine has been reduced by half, add the juice of one lemon.

➡ Add salt and pepper to taste, then remove from heat and swirl in butter until it is incorporated completely.

➡ Pour sauce over piccata slices, then scatter crispy capers and the parsley on top. Cut one lemon in wedges and place them attractively around all.

VARIATIONS
Boneless skinless chicken breasts or pork loin, sliced and pounded, may be used instead of turkey.

MENU IDEAS
Serve this dish with "Uncle Scrooge's Golden Risotto."

Figaro's
TROUT IN CRAZY WATER

A tiny ball of black-and-white fur totally devoted to his master, Geppetto, this engaging kitten demands constant attention. Figaro generally gets his way, which is clear in the scene where his master cooks a trout just for him. Low in calories, big on flavor, this simply cooked and presented fish does, however, demand some attention of its own. After a delicious dinner like this, the least a kid could do would be to open the window—just as Figaro does in the film *Pinocchio*—gaze up, and thank the wishing star for having a parent as loving as you.

> **LOOK AT HIM, FIGARO: HE ALMOST LOOKS ALIVE!**

HOW TO MAKE IT

4 Servings

2 Preparation Time (hours)

INGREDIENTS

1 quart	water
2 cups	dry white wine
1	onion, sliced
1	bay leaf
2 sprigs	thyme
6 sprigs	parsley
2	hot chili peppers, split
1	carrot, sliced
1 rib	celery, sliced
	salt to taste
4	whole small trout, head on
1	lemon, sliced
1	roasted red pepper, cut into strips
4	olives, large, stuffed with pimiento

➡ Heat water, wine, onion, bay leaf, thyme, 2 sprigs of parsley, hot peppers, carrots, celery, and salt in a large deep roasting pan, preferably one with a rack.

➡ Bring to a boil; cook for about 15 minutes and taste (broth should be very strongly flavored).

➡ Meanwhile, rinse and dry whole trout. Using butcher's twine, gently tie the tail to the head of the fish so that it forms a U shape. Place trout in simmering broth (your pan will probably hold only 2 at a time), and add water if the tops of the fish aren't covered. Partially cover pan and cook for about 15 minutes at a very low simmer—there should be no movement of broth, no visible bubbles.

➡ Carefully remove fish by lifting rack if there is one; if not, use a large flat spatula. Place fish on a platter and cover with foil, and hold in warm oven while the remaining fish are cooking.

➡ Using scissors, carefully remove the string but keep the U shape and place on a platter. Decorate with the sliced lemons, roasted red pepper strips, olives, and remaining parsley sprigs.

NUTRITION INFORMATION

Each Serving Contains

Calories	499
Total fat	11 g
Saturated fat	1 g
Sodium	657 mg
Carbohydrates	58 g
Fiber	12 g
Protein	40 g

SERVING SUGGESTIONS

Serve individual trout portions in large soup bowls, with some of the strained cooking liquid as gravy, and boiled potatoes on the side.

MENU IDEAS

Start off with "Alice's Warm Mushroom Salad" and finish with "Winnie the Pooh's No-Bake Honey Cookies."

NOTES

Halibut or salmon steaks may be substituted for trout, if desired. Adjust the cooking times accordingly.

WHAT CHILDREN CAN DO

Children can decorate the completed dish with sliced lemons, red pepper strips, and olives.

Oliver & Company's
from Oliver & Company

DRY-ROASTED CHICKEN

This meal's origins are as humble as those of Oliver, yet from a lowly bulb—garlic, of course—and a simple bird—the ubiquitous chicken—springs a dish worthy of elegant, urbane settings. And just as Oliver, through his kind demeanor and youthful innocence, melts the hearts of Fagin and his gang, the sumptuous simplicity here is sure to win over even your most finicky guests. Who knows—such a display of cooking talent might end up getting you "adopted" (as Oliver was by Jenny) . . . that is, if you aren't already spoken for.

66 WAIT TILL YOU TASTE THIS. IT'S A SECRET RECIPE I JUST INVENTED! 99

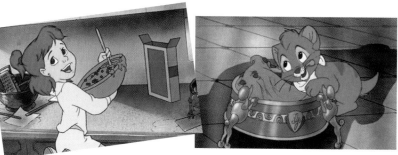

HOW TO MAKE IT

4	Servings
3	Preparation Time (hours)

INGREDIENTS

4 heads	garlic
2 tbs.	chopped thyme
1/2 tsp.	salt
1/4 tsp.	pepper
4 lb.	chicken, whole
2	bay leaves
4 sprigs	thyme
3	lemons
1 tb.	chopped parsley

NUTRITION INFORMATION

Each Serving Contains

Calories	604
Total fat	25 g
Saturated fat	616 g
Sodium	514 mg
Carbohydrate	16 g
Fiber	1 g
Protein	82 g

➡ Preheat oven to 350°F. Rub some of the excess skin from heads of garlic; wrap loosely in foil. Roast in preheated oven until softened and smelling like roasted nuts, about 1 hour. Remove from foil, and let cool.

➡ Cut the top of each head and squeeze out the roasted garlic onto a cutting board. With the side of a chef's knife, mash cloves on cutting board until a smooth paste is formed. This may be covered with a thin film of olive oil and stored in the refrigerator for several days.

➡ Mix garlic paste with the 2 tbs. of chopped thyme, salt, and pepper. Wash and dry chicken. With your fingers, separate the skin from the chicken starting at the top of the breast, and continuing until you have reached the leg/thigh joint.

➡ With a teaspoon, carefully place roasted garlic mixture under the skin, then wash your hands. Now massage the chicken to distribute the mixture evenly under the skin.

➡ Stuff chicken with bay leaves, sprigs of thyme, and one lemon, cut in quarters. With string, tie legs together so that the bird roasts evenly and looks more attractive when served.

➡ You may prepare this 1 day in advance. Store *unwrapped* in refrigerator to allow skin to dry somewhat.

➡ Roast chicken in a preheated 350°F oven. The chicken is done when the internal temperature has reached 165°F, or when juices run clear when thigh joint is pierced with a fork, about 1 1/2 hours cooking time.

➡ Broil halved lemons until attractively charred, to use as garnish. Top with chopped parsley and juices from cutting board.

VARIATIONS

If you don't want to roast a whole chicken, you can use boneless breast of chicken, stuffing the mixture under the skin in the same way, whether cooking for a large party or for just one serving.

MENU IDEAS

Serve "Fun and Fancy Free's Ratatouille" alongside, and perhaps some simple roasted potatoes to complete the dish.

WHAT CHILDREN CAN DO

Kids can remove excess skin from garlic and mash roasted cloves in a metal mixing bowl with the back of a spoon.

King Hubert's
from Sleeping Beauty

VEAL ROAST WITH APRICOTS AND THYME

his is a dish fit for a king—or a queen. Your table should be laid out in regal fashion as you serve up this delicate veal roast, braised in fruity wine with aromatic herbs and Turkish apricots until meltingly tender. Imagine King Hubert himself at the head of the table, licking his chops as he celebrates the marriage and other milestones of his child's life on this monumental occasion! You can bet he would approve of such downright royal delights.

> " TONIGHT, WE TOAST THE FUTURE . . . WITH SOMETHING I'VE BEEN SAVING FOR SIXTEEN YEARS. "

HOW TO MAKE IT

4 Servings

4 Preparation Time (hours)

INGREDIENTS

1 tb.	olive oil
4 oz.	shallots, peeled and sliced
3 lb.	veal bottom round, rolled and tied
$^1/_2$ tsp.	salt
$^1/_2$ tsp.	white pepper
$^1/_2$ bunch	thyme
2	bay leaves
$^1/_4$ bunch	parsley, tied up
2 cups	white wine, Gewürztraminer
1 quart	chicken broth, hot
4 oz.	dried apricot halves, coarsely chopped
1 tb.	chopped parsley

NUTRITION INFORMATION

Each Serving Contains

Calories	469
Total fat	10 g
Saturated fat	3 g
Sodium	1,212 mg
Carbohydrates	35 g
Fiber	4 g
Protein	42 g

➡ Heat oil in a nonstick pan with lid. When hot, add shallots and sauté until lightly browned; then remove. Add veal roast and brown well on all sides; then season with salt and pepper. Add thyme, bay leaves, parsley, wine, and shallots and bring to a boil.

➡ Boil for 2 to 3 minutes to burn off alcohol. Add chicken broth and return to a boil; then reduce to a slow simmer. Cook, partially covered, for about 2 hours, turning the meat every 30 minutes. As the meat cooks, add chicken broth as needed to keep the veal half covered with liquid.

➡ Uncover after 2 hours and remove the bunches of parsley and thyme. Add apricots and continue cooking, uncovered, at a low simmer until meat is tender. Your roast should be easily pierced with a knife after about 20 to 30 additional minutes. Total cooking time should be approximately $2^1/_2$ hours.

➡ Remove meat and place on a cutting board for about 15 minutes before carving. Puree one quarter of the sauce, and pour back into the pot. Adjust salt and pepper to taste. If sauce appears too thick, add more broth; if too thin, boil off a portion of the water. Slice meat and lightly dress with sauce. Garnish with chopped parsley.

NOTES

The entire dish can be prepared a day or two in advance. In fact, this will improve its flavor. If this is your plan, leave the meat whole in the sauce, cooking it a bit less, since you will be reheating it. Reheat gently in sauce and slice just before serving, garnishing with cooked apricots in a pool of sauce.

MENU IDEAS

A salad with "Bambi and Thumper's Green Goddess Dressing" would be a fresh and crisp start to this meal of regal proportions. For a fitting end, try "The Rescuers' Sweet Potato Pie with Cheese."

WHAT CHILDREN CAN DO

Kids can tie the parsley up with cooking strings.

King Midas's

from The Golden Touch

HAMBURGER STUFFED WITH GOLDEN ONIONS

t times we all long for that mythical genie or elf who will grant us three magic wishes. Midas got his wish, and everything he touched turned to gold. Even his food turned to gold, which, alas, he could not eat. He finally persuaded Goldie, the magical elf who granted him this wish, to remove this "curse" when he agreed to forsake all his worldly possessions. At the end of the movie we see Midas stripped down to his drawers, but beaming with joy as he enjoys one of life's simplest pleasures, a perfectly cooked hamburger, loaded with "golden onions." So, without further ado, here's the recipe for this simple, soul-satisfying feast. One word of advice, though: be careful what you wish for. . . .

> **" MY GOLD, MY KINGDOM FOR A HAMBURGER SANDWICH! JUST PLAIN OLD HAMBURGER! "**

HOW TO MAKE IT

4 Servings

1 Preparation Time (hours)

INGREDIENTS

1 lb.	onions, peeled
$\frac{1}{4}$ cup	olive oil
1 tsp.	chopped parsley
$\frac{1}{2}$ tsp.	salt
$\frac{1}{4}$ tsp.	freshly ground black pepper
$1\frac{1}{2}$ lb.	ground chuck
2 tbs.	Worcestershire sauce
4	mixed-grain hamburger buns

NUTRITION INFORMATION

Each Serving Contains

Calories	716
Total fat	52 g
Saturated fat	17 g
Sodium	1,087 mg
Carbohydrates	25 g
Fiber	4 g
Protein	35 g

➡ Slice onions thickly. Slowly sauté, uncovered, in olive oil in a nonstick pan until caramelized, 15–20 minutes.

➡ Remove from heat and add parsley, salt, and pepper; this is best done the day before, allowing excess oil to drain off.

➡ Mix ground chuck with Worcestershire sauce and divide into 8 patties.

➡ Divide onion mixture into 4 portions and place in the center of 4 patties.

➡ Cover with the remaining 4 patties, carefully sealing to make sure that no onions are exposed, as you squeeze out any air from the centers.

➡ Preheat grill, broiler, or nonstick pan until very hot. Cook burgers without moving for about 7 minutes.

➡ Flip and cook an additional 5 to 6 minutes for medium-rare, 6 to 7 minutes for medium, or 7 to 8 minutes for medium well-done. Toast buns and serve with hamburgers.

VARIATIONS

When in a hurry, serve the onions on top of the burger, along with toasted buns.

SERVING SUGGESTIONS

Garnish with lettuce, sliced tomatoes, ketchup, mayonnaise, mustard, and pickles to start. The rest is up to you.

WHAT CHILDREN CAN DO

With parental supervision, little hands can shape the hamburgers before they are cooked.

Simba's

from The Lion King

SEARED FILLET OF BEEF

imba was sure lucky to meet up with pals like Pumbaa and Timon, just when he needed friends most. Alongside them, he grew up to be the courageous King of the Savannah we know today. About the only thing he never shared with his buddies was their predilection for grubs and other creepy-crawlies. That's why we've dedicated this tender beef filet to him. It provides a wallop of taste and substance for anyone who needs the strength and stamina of a lion.

" ANY ANTELOPE . . . ? HIPPO? "

HOW TO MAKE IT

4 Servings

45 Preparation Time (minutes)

INGREDIENTS

1 tsp.	ground cumin
¹/₂ tsp.	ground cinnamon
¹/₂ tsp.	salt
¹/₂ tsp.	cayenne pepper
¹/₂ tsp.	sugar
1 lb. (4 portions)	beef tenderloin, trimmed of all fat, center cut
1 lb.	spinach, washed and stemmed
3 tbs.	olive oil
1	onion, thinly sliced
	salt and pepper to taste
2 oz.	peanuts, roasted and crushed
1	lemon, cut in 4 wedges

➡ Combine ground cumin, cinnamon, salt, cayenne pepper, and sugar; then use to coat the four pieces of tenderloin.

➡ Heat a cast-iron pan until very hot. Wash spinach and drain well.

➡ Heat 2 tablespoons olive oil in a nonstick pan until very hot. Sauté sliced onion until brown and beginning to crisp, about 10–12 minutes.

➡ Coat hot cast-iron skillet lightly with 1 tablespoon olive oil.

➡ Cook steaks on one side, without moving, for about 5 minutes; then flip and cook an additional 4 minutes. Remove from pan and set aside while finishing garnish.

➡ When onions are done, remove from oil, and drain on a paper towel–lined plate.

➡ Place cleaned spinach in same pan onions were cooked in. Cover and cook with only the residual water on leaves. Remove cover after 1 to 2 minutes, and flip spinach until just wilted. Season to taste with salt and pepper.

➡ Divide fried onions and spinach evenly among 4 plates. Place a fillet partially over each spinach portion, pouring any accumulated juices onto the meat. Sprinkle with roasted peanuts and garnish with a wedge of lemon.

NUTRITION INFORMATION

Each Serving Contains

Calories	524
Total fat	44 g
Saturated fat	13 g
Carbohydrates	11 g
Sodium	528 mg
Fiber	48 g
Protein	27 g

VARIATIONS
Use chicken breasts instead of beef. Also various mixed greens can replace spinach, though cooking time is usually a bit longer.

SERVING SUGGESTIONS
This dish is particularly attractive when served on simple, heavy earthenware plates, with wooden-handled steak knives.

MENU IDEAS
Begin this meal with a bowl of "Cinderella's Herb and Egg White Soup" and finish up with "Tigger's Frozen Dark Chocolate Orange Mousse."

WHAT CHILDREN CAN DO
Children can wash spinach and crush peanuts.

Mulan's

from Mulan

MAHOGANY CHICKEN

Y ou don't meet a girl like that . . . every dynasty."
And though the courageous maiden who defeated the Huns
and saved the Chinese Empire is not particularly versatile
when it come to household chores, rest assured that even
Mulan, perhaps with the help of Grandmother Fa, would
be able to prepare this scrumptious spicy chicken bursting
with Oriental fragrances. Strong, tender, and definitely
nonconformist—just like Mulan herself—this dish is well
worth a trip to your nearest Asian grocery to stock up
on all the exotic ingredients necessary. If Mulan's Mahogany
Chicken doesn't arouse your ancient ancestors, don't worry—
they're probably attending to more important business.

**" FULFILL YOUR DUTIES
CALMLY AND RESPECTFULLY.
REFLECT BEFORE
YOU SNACK . . . UHM . . . ACT! "**

HOW TO MAKE IT

4 Servings

1½ Preparation Time (days)

INGREDIENTS

6 tbs.	hoisin sauce*
6 tbs.	plum sauce*
¼ cup	soy sauce
¼ cup	apple cider vinegar
¼ cup	dry sherry
¼ cup	blackstrap* molasses
3½–4 lb.	chicken, whole
2 tsps.	Szechuan* peppercorns,
3	thinly sliced scallions

*These items are available at Asian markets.

NUTRITION INFORMATION

Each Serving Contains

Calories	578
Total fat	21 g
Saturated fat	6 g
Sodium	1,014 mg
Carbohydrates	29 g
Fiber	2 g
Protein	61 g

➡ Combine all ingredients except chicken, peppercorns, and scallions, mixing well.

➡ Wash and dry chicken and place in plastic bag; then pour marinade into the bag, squeezing out as much air as possible. Refrigerate overnight.

➡ The following day, preheat oven to 300°F. Drain chicken, discarding marinade. Place chicken, breast side up, on a roasting rack. Tie legs for a more attractive roast, then place in oven, uncovered. The chicken is done when the internal temperature has reached 165°F, about 1½ hours, or when juices run clear when thigh joint is pierced with a fork.

➡ Remove from oven and let stand 15 minutes before carving. Place peppercorns in a small dry skillet over high heat, shaking constantly for several minutes, until they are fragrant. Remove from pan and crush with a mortar and pestle.

➡ Carve chicken to serve, saving any accumulated juices. Garnish with sliced scallions and peppercorns.

VARIATIONS

Use this same marinade on pork chops to be roasted, or with Cornish hens for a more formal dinner.

MENU IDEAS

Begin with with "Si and Am's Appetizers," and accompany the entrée with steamed rice and sautéed snow peas. For dessert, a slice of "Maid Marian's Blackberry Pie" would be in order.

Pecos Bill's

GRILLED RIB-EYE STEAK WITH RED-EYE GRAVY

ecos Bill and his trusted steed Widowmaker belong to a page of American folklore when men were men and the Wild West was still as wild as the great outdoors. Raised by a family of coyotes, the blond-haired, blue-eyed Bill rides tall in his saddle, working up a hearty appetite out on the range. Indeed, when a drought strikes Texas, he personally lassos a rain cloud from as far away as California and hauls it in for some watery relief. Any man who works this hard deserves some serious "grub," and an all-American rib-eye steak with a modern red-eye gravy should fit the bill nicely.

" WHEN HE LET OUT A YELL, THERE WAS NOTHING THAT WOULD STAND UP TO HIM; HE COULD FRIGHTEN AWAY A TREACHEROUS TWISTER, OR SCARE A CACTUS INTO LOSING ITS PRICKERS! "

HOW TO MAKE IT

4 Servings

45 Preparation Time
(minutes)

INGREDIENTS

¹/₄ cup	ground coffee
¹/₄ cup	freshly ground black pepper
2 tbs.	salt
¹/₄ cup	brown sugar
4 (6 oz. each)	rib-eye steaks
1 tb.	olive oil
²/₃ cup	water

NUTRITION INFORMATION

Each Serving Contains

Calories	589
Total fat	43 g
Saturated fat	18 g
Sodium	1,709 mg
Carbohydrates	143 g
Fiber	1 g
Protein	41 g

➡ Combine coffee, pepper, salt, and brown sugar. Rub steaks with half the mixture and marinate 30 minutes, keeping the rest of the dry rub in a tightly sealed jar in the refrigerator.

➡ When ready to cook, heat a cast-iron skillet, large enough to hold all the steaks without crowding, until extremely hot.

➡ Film the pan with olive oil; then place in steaks and immediately turn down heat. Watch the sides of steaks for cooking times: for medium steaks, flip over once the color along the sides of the meat changes halfway up; then continue cooking on the other side for a somewhat shorter period of time (4 to 5 minutes as opposed to, say, 6 minutes). Well-done steaks should cook on the first side until color is three quarters of the way up; then flip and continue to cook for a bit less time. For rare steaks, cook until color change on the side is just one quarter of the way up; then flip and cook for slightly less time.

➡ When done to your liking, remove steaks to a platter. Let stand for a few minutes before serving.

➡ Add ²/₃ cup water to the pan you cooked the steaks in and bring to a boil. With a wooden spoon, scrape up any bits stuck to the bottom of the pan. Reduce by boiling down to half. Adjust for salt. Pour sauce over steaks and serve.

NOTES
This dry rub works best when sautéed in a pan, as opposed to cooking on an open grill.

MENU IDEAS
Serve this dish alongside "The Three Little Pigs' Potato Pancakes with Applesauce" for a hearty and satisfying meal.

WHAT CHILDREN CAN DO

Kids can mix brown sugar, salt, coffee, and black pepper for the dry rub.

Peg Leg Pete's

from Shanghaied

SEARED SWORDFISH WITH MINT BREAD-CRUMB SAUCE

I n the 1934 short movie Shanghaied, *skipper Peg Leg Pete and his look-alike crew of pirates captured and bound Minnie and Mickey in ropes. Mickey escaped and saved Minnie by dueling Peg Leg Pete with a stuffed swordfish. Mickey repeatedly landed his sword in Peg Leg Pete's posterior, a tactic that led him to victory and saved the day. Vanquished Pete was punished severely and made an example of to one and all. To console this eternal loser, and to provide a not-so-subtle allusion to his downfall, we've come up with a swordfish recipe that's out of this world, transforming the means that procured his humiliation into a delicious dish that will have everybody licking their chops. One taste of this and Pete himself might turn into a "good guy."*

66 HULLO, SWEETIE. HOW ABOUT A KISS FOR POPPA? 99

HOW TO MAKE IT

4 Servings

1 Preparation Time (hours)

INGREDIENTS

3 tbs.	fresh bread crumbs, white part only
1 bunch	mint leaves, finely chopped
2	shallots, finely chopped
$\frac{1}{2}$ cup	rice-wine vinegar
$\frac{1}{4}$ tsp.	salt
$\frac{1}{8}$ tsp.	pepper
1 oz.	olive oil
1 lb. (4 oz. each)	swordfish steaks

NUTRITION INFORMATION

Each Serving Contains

Calories	286
Total fat	13 g
Saturated fat	3 g
Sodium	363 mg
Carbohydrates	17 g
Fiber	1 g
Protein	25 g

➡ Preheat oven to 350°F. Toast bread crumbs until dry but not browned, then let cool. Add mint leaves and shallots to bread crumbs; then add vinegar, salt, and pepper, and mix. Mixture should have the texture of wet sand. Set aside at room temperature while cooking fish, for no more than 30 minutes.

➡ Heat a nonstick sauté pan until very hot (it should be big enough to hold all 4 pieces of fish comfortably). Swirl oil to coat.

➡ Place swordfish steaks in pan when oil begins to smoke. Sear for 3 to 4 minutes, watching color change on sides. When color has changed halfway up, flip and cook the second side a bit less than the first. Place steaks on plate and garnish with a portion of sauce.

NOTES
Other solid white-flesh fish may be used, such as halibut, sturgeon, or even squid steaks.

MENU IDEAS
"Gus the Goose's Spaghetti with Peas" would be a simple appetizer for this dish. Follow up with a portion of "Mowgli's Mixed Vegetable Salad" and a plate of "Santa's Cookies" for dessert.

WHAT CHILDREN CAN DO

Kids can pluck mint leaves from stems.

Pluto's

from Cold Turkey

COLD ROAST TURKEY BREAST

In the 1951 short movie Cold Turkey, Pluto and Milton the cat are two housemates who live in relative harmony. A TV commercial for Lurkey's Turkeys sets their mouths watering, and both come up with the same idea: Why not roast one of those birds themselves? Too bad their methods are debatable, to say the least. Your best bet here is to intervene as little as possible, letting the oven handle most of the work. This recipe is easier than traditional roast turkey, perfect for smaller families. While a whole bird is shown in the movie, I have opted for a boneless breast of turkey, which will be enough for dinner and sandwiches as well.

"DON'T WORRY, PLUTO— YOU'RE A BETTER DOG THAN ANY OF THEM!"

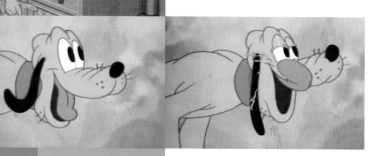

HOW TO MAKE IT

8 Servings

1½ Preparation Time (days)

INGREDIENTS

6 lb.	boneless turkey breast
2 cups	dried cranberries, coarsely chopped
½ bunch	minced thyme
½ cup	white wine
½ tsp.	freshly ground black pepper
1 tsp.	mustard seeds
3 tsps.	finely chopped candied gingerroot
1 small	hot pepper, finely chopped
½ small	onion, finely chopped
	salt and pepper to taste

NUTRITION INFORMATION

Each Serving Contains

Calories	513
Total fat	22 g
Saturated fat	6 g
Sodium	217 mg
Carbohydrates	4 g
Fiber	1 g
Protein	68 g

➡ Have your butcher bone, roll, and tie a breast of turkey, instructing him not to roll it too tightly, as you'll be stuffing it with a cranberry mixture.

➡ Combine all ingredients except turkey in a pot and cook until most of the liquid has evaporated, being careful not to scorch the bottom of the pot. Remove pot from heat and allow to cool. This stuffing may be made up to several days in advance and kept refrigerated.

➡ Before stuffing turkey breast, remove ½ cup of the cranberry mixture and set aside. Carefully stuff turkey breast, using your fingers and the back end of a wooden spoon. After stuffing, wipe turkey breast clean, season with salt and pepper, wrap in plastic, and marinate in refrigerator overnight.

➡ The following day, preheat oven to 325°F. For roasting times, calculate 14 minutes per pound, or until an instant-read thermometer shows 165°F. After removing from oven, allow turkey to stand for 2 hours at room temperature before refrigerating, uncovered, until completely cold. Only at this point should it be wrapped in plastic.

➡ When serving, slice thinner than you normally would for hot portions.

NOTES

The remaining cranberry sauce may be mixed with a combination of mayonnaise and a dab of sour cream or créme fraîche for a nice cold sauce.

VARIATIONS

This same stuffing can be used with pork loin. Have your butcher make a hole down the center of the pork loin with a sharpening steel; then stuff as you would with turkey. Roast at 350°F until an instant-read thermometer inserted in the middle shows 145°F. Make a sauce out of the drippings combined with the remaining cranberry stuffing.

SERVING SUGGESTIONS

This turkey breast may also be served hot, and is great for a holiday buffet since there are no bones and it is very easy to slice. Garnish with pan drippings mixed with the remaining cranberry stuffing, adding salt and pepper to taste.

Quasimodo's

MULTICOLORED CABBAGE SALAD AND CHICKEN

uasimodo is an artist—remember his finely sculpted and painted statuettes of characters from his world? Well, here's a chance to express your own artistic flair as you put together a culinary composition of shapes and colors. The multicolored cabbage salad is similar to the glass mobile that first enticed Esmeralda to enter the bell tower for closer inspection. The dressing is subtle and alluring, slightly sweet and sharp, as only Esmeralda can be. The black pepper in the marinade represents Frollo, the dark, complex figure, both sharp and strong at the same time, thinking he does no wrong. When they're all combined, we have a complex dish representing the three main characters of this unforgettable story.

> **I AM NEVER TOO BUSY TO SHARE A MEAL WITH YOU, DEAR BOY. I BROUGHT A LITTLE . . . TREAT.**

HOW TO MAKE IT

4 Servings

2 Preparation Time (hours)

INGREDIENTS

CHICKEN

$\frac{1}{2}$	lemon, zest and juice
2 tsps.	black peppercorns, crushed
2 tbs.	leaf oregano
$\frac{1}{4}$ cup	extra-virgin olive oil
$\frac{1}{2}$ tsp.	salt
$\frac{1}{2}$ bunch	scallions, sliced
4 tbs.	chopped parsley
4 (6 oz. each)	skinless, boneless chicken breasts

CABBAGE SALAD

$\frac{1}{4}$ cup	extra-virgin olive oil
$\frac{1}{4}$ cup	apple cider vinegar
1 tb.	orange zest
4 tbs.	chopped parsley
$\frac{1}{2}$ can	frozen orange-juice concentrate
$\frac{1}{2}$ tsp.	black pepper
$\frac{1}{4}$ tsp.	salt
1 lb.	green cabbage, shredded
$\frac{1}{2}$ lb.	red cabbage, shredded
$\frac{1}{2}$	green bell pepper
$\frac{1}{2}$	red bell pepper

CHICKEN

➡ Grate the zest from the lemon and place in a large glass bowl; then add its juice. Add black pepper, oregano, olive oil, salt, sliced scallions, and chopped parsley; the mixture will be very thick.

➡ Rub mixture onto both sides of chicken breasts, marinating a minimum of $\frac{1}{2}$ hour. When ready to cook, place on hot grill. Allow about 4 minutes per side, turning only once.

➡ Spoon cabbage salad onto serving platter; place grilled chicken on top. Do not drain cabbage salad of any accumulated juices. Garnish with chopped parsley.

CABBAGE SALAD

➡ Combine oil, vinegar, orange zest, parsley, orange-juice concentrate, pepper, and salt. Sauce should be sweet and sour, with an orange flavor.

➡ Add shredded cabbages and bell peppers. Hold at room temperature for no longer than 1 hour before serving, or refrigerate for up to 2 hours.

NUTRITIONAL INFORMATION

Each Serving Contains

Calories	861
Total fat	35 g
Saturated fat	4 g
Sodium	1,369 mg
Carbohydrates	102 g
Fiber	15 g
Protein	64 g

SERVING SUGGESTIONS

Serve with a side of rice pilaf made from white, brown, and wild rice.

VARIATIONS

Replace boneless chicken with 1 whole chicken cut into eighths. The recipe is the same, though cooking time is a bit longer.

WHAT CHILDREN CAN DO

Little hands can mix the cabbage salad for the base of this dish.

The Scat Cat Band's

CRISPY FRIED SOLE FILLETS WITH RAW TOMATO SAUCE

*I*f Scat Cat and his band have one thing, it's soul! That's why I've come up with these crispy sole fillets, accompanied by a sensual flourish of tomatoes with a bit of garlic for zip and olive oil for the transitional notes—dig? The right place to enjoy them would surely be a brightly painted Bohemian attic in Paris, though I'm quite confident that this entrée will win over guests wherever you happen to call home. Just remember to pop on some cool jazz—then kick back for a hip soiree.

" OH, HO-HO, YOU ARE CHARMING. AND YOUR MUSIC IS SO . . . SO DIFFERENT, AH, SO EXCITING . . ."
"IT ISN'T BEETHOVEN, MAMA, BUT IT SURE BOUNCES! "

HOW TO MAKE IT

4 Servings

1¼ Preparation Time (hours)

INGREDIENTS

1 lb.	Roma tomatoes, ripest available
2 cloves	garlic, finely chopped
4 tbs.	extra-virgin olive oil
6	basil leaves, chopped
	salt and pepper to taste
1 lb.	sole fillets
2 oz.	flour
2	eggs, beaten
2 tbs.	water
4 oz.	fresh bread crumbs
1 tb.	dried oregano, crushed
6 tbs.	olive oil

➡ Cut tomatoes in half and remove seeds. Coarsely chop and place in a glass bowl. Add garlic, extra-virgin olive oil, basil, and salt and pepper to taste, marinating at room temperature for up to 1 hour. When ready to cook, season sole fillets with salt and pepper to taste.

➡ Place flour in a bowl. In another bowl, combine eggs and water, and mix well. Combine fresh bread crumbs and dried oregano in a third bowl.

➡ Heat a nonstick sauté pan until hot. Add olive oil, and heat to 350°F.

➡ Dip sole in flour, shake off excess, coat thoroughly with egg mixture, then cover with bread crumbs. This can be done while pan and oil are heating up. Sauté until light golden brown on first side; turn and cook second side until same color.

➡ Keep fish warm until ready to serve, on a paper towel-lined plate. Serve with raw tomato sauce (no lemon, please).

NUTRITION INFORMATION

Each Serving Contains

Calories	350
Total fat	41 g
Saturated fat	6 g
Carbohydrates	32 g
Sodium	289 mg
Fiber	3 g
Protein	25 g

NOTES

Other fish fillets may easily be substituted for sole, as long as they are no more than ½ inch thick. The sauce is also good mixed room temperature with hot pasta, which is then served without grated cheese.

MENU IDEAS

Begin this meal with a small bowl of "Cinderella's Herb and Egg White Soup."

WHAT CHILDREN CAN DO

Kids love to crush tomatoes with their hands!

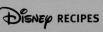

Sir Ector's

from The Sword in the Stone

WHISKEY-GLAZED HAM

Sir Ector, foster father of Wart, enjoyed nothing more than inviting distinguished guests to his castle in Forest Sauvage for sumptuous feasts, where the wine flowed freely. Here then is a recipe for glazed ham that would surely be a hit even at a royal banquet which I'm certain your family and friends will love, too. From his girth, it looks like Sir Ector gobbled up the entire feast by himself, perhaps conceding a morsel or two to his son, Sir Kay, or his friend Sir Pelinore. But Sir Ector does have a heart: indeed, he was one of the first to acknowledge Wart's ability to remove the sword from the stone. Who knows, after dining on this luscious ham, perhaps you, too, will have the strength needed to remove your own sword from the stone!

" HERE'S TO LONDON! AND HERE'S TO KAY! AND HERE'S TO THE BANNER OF THE CASTLE OF THE FOREST SAUVAGE! "

HOW TO MAKE IT

12 Servings

2½ Preparation Time (hours)

INGREDIENTS

5 lb.	smoked ham, fully cooked
2 tbs.	cloves, whole
1 pint	whiskey
1 cup	honey
¼ cup	molasses
½ tsp.	ground coriander
½ tsp.	ground nutmeg

NUTRITION INFORMATION

Each Serving Contains

Calories	511
Total fat	20 g
Saturated fat	7 g
Carbohydrates	26 g
Sodium	2,125 mg
Fiber	1 g
Protein	33 g

➡ Preheat oven to 325°F. Rinse and dry smoked ham, then stud it with whole cloves, inserting the thin pointed end into the meat, with the "flower end" exposed on the outside. Place in an ovenproof roasting pan and allow to stand at room temperature while you prepare the glaze.

➡ Combine remaining ingredients in a saucepan, and bring to a boil. Reduce by about ⅓ volume, which should take about 10 minutes. If dish flares up, don't worry; it's the alcohol from the whiskey burning off. This is normal, but be careful.

➡ Brush ⅓ of the marinade over ham, cover loosely with foil, then place in preheated oven. Baste ham with accumulated juices and extra liquid, as needed, approximately every 20 minutes, for a total of 1½ hours.

➡ If ham needs more browning, turn heat up to 400°F and baste with any accumulated juices every 10 minutes just to brown the skin. Keep a close eye on it to avoid burning. Remove to a platter. Cool about 20 minutes before slicing.

SERVING SUGGESTIONS

Be unconventional by serving this ham with the carving knife sticking out of it, to represent the Sword in the Stone. Select a King Arthur to remove it and do the carving for one and all.

MENU IDEAS

A bowl of "Snow White's Winter Vegetable Soup" would be perfect before enjoying a plate of this ham.

WHAT CHILDREN CAN DO

Kids can push the cloves into the ham in attractive patterns, perhaps while discussing the legend of King Arthur. Also, when making this recipe for children, replace whiskey with apple-juice concentrate.

Ichabod's ROAST TURKEY WITH GIBLET GRAVY

from The Adventures of Ichabod and Mr. Toad

A much anticipated Thanksgiving ritual, roast turkey is the classic American dish. It's definitely one of Ichabod's favorites, especially when prepared by the mother of one of his students. She is particularly adept at turning out an excellent bird, as the gourmet of old once noted in his diary. Don't ask how we got our hands on this recipe, but we'll gladly pass it on to you. A couple things, though: try not to lose your head over this dish the way Ichabod does, and save room for a slice of pumpkin pie afterward. Too bad the Headless Horseman never got a chance to try some—I'm sure he would have cooled his jets if Ichabod had only thought to offer him a succulent drumstick.

❝ DON'T STOP TO FIGURE OUT A PLAN. YOU CAN'T REASON WITH A HEADLESS MAN! ❞

HOW TO MAKE IT

12 Servings

1½ Preparation Time (days)

INGREDIENTS

10 lb.	turkey, whole
2 tbs.	onion powder
1 tsp.	garlic powder
1 tsp.	thyme
1 tb.	salt
½ tsp.	black pepper
1 tsp.	sugar
3	bay leaves
3 tbs.	sage
½ cup	olive oil
3	carrots, split lengthwise
6 ribs	celery, whole
2	onions, quartered
6 oz.	cherry tomatoes
2 yards	cheesecloth
4 tbs.	flour
1 bunch	chopped parsley
1 quart	water

NUTRITION INFORMATION
Each Serving Contains

Calories	529
Total fat	25 g
Saturated fat	7 g
Sodium	867 mg
Carbohydrates	11 g
Fiber	2 g
Protein	63 g

➡ Remove giblets from turkey and set them aside. Wash and dry the bird well.

➡ Marinade: Mix a bit of water, onion powder, garlic powder, thyme, salt, pepper, sugar, bay leaves, and sage in a food processor or blender until smooth. Add ¼ cup of olive oil, and process for an additional 10 seconds.

➡ Place carrots, celery, onions, and tomatoes in the bottom of roasting pan, which will keep the turkey out of its own drippings while cooking and help make wonderful gravy.

➡ Place turkey on vegetables in roasting pan, rubbing marinade both inside and outside turkey.

➡ Use butcher's twine to tie legs together for even roasting and an attractive presentation. Fold wing joints under breast and place pan on bottom shelf of refrigerator *uncovered*. Marinate overnight.

➡ Remove pan with turkey and vegetables from fridge about 1 hour before cooking. Preheat oven to 325°F. Open cheesecloth, soak completely in remaining ¼ cup of olive oil in small mixing bowl.

➡ Cover the bird with this "shroud," making sure that the whole turkey is covered and that nothing is hanging out of the pan. Roast in oven for 2¼ to 2¾ hours. There's no need to baste with this method.

➡ Rinse giblets (no liver) and place in a pot with 1 quart of water, bring to a boil, reduce to a simmer, and cook for 1½ hours.

➡ Check turkey after 2¼ hours with an instant-read thermometer inserted at leg/thigh joint. Turkey is done when temperature has reached 165°F and juices run clear.

WHAT CHILDREN CAN DO

Kids can mix the marinade for the turkey and wash the carrots, celery, and onions before they are placed in the bottom of the roasting pan. They can also sprinkle parsley over the cooked turkey and decorate it with cherry tomatoes.

HOW TO MAKE IT

Continue roasting until indicated temperature is reached. When turkey is done, remove to a platter. Cover loosely with foil to keep warm, with cheesecloth intact.

➡ Place roasting pan on a large burner, sauté vegetables until caramelized, breaking them up as you do so, about 15 minutes. Add enough flour with a wooden spoon to make a roux with the texture of wet sand (several tablespoons); cook an additional 5 to 10 minutes.

➡ Remove giblets from stock and finely dice. Set aside for gravy.

➡ Pour stock into roasting pan. Continue to mix well while cooking (may be somewhat lumpy).

➡ Add salt and pepper to taste. Continue cooking until slightly thickened, with a smooth, creamy texture. Strain gravy, discard solids, then add diced giblets, plus salt and pepper to taste.

➡ Now, slowly peel cheesecloth off turkey and pour any accumulated juices into the gravy. Untie legs, serve gravy alongside.

➡ Sprinkle the finished roasted turkey with chopped parsley and place the cherry tomatoes around the base of the turkey before serving.

Salads, Dressings, and Sandwiches

Alice's WARM MUSHROOM SALAD

from Alice in Wonderland

Alice, a proper English girl, gets a hot tip on the magical powers of Wonderland mushrooms from the Caterpillar, but you won't have to worry about your waist changing size after eating this dish. This simple but eye-catching recipe will add a touch of originality to a more elaborate meal. Taking a cue from the multicolor garden Alice crosses, create a fine flowery decoration—edible, not talking, flowers, that is! Follow each step carefully, and your guests will be overcome by the "magic spell" of this mushroom salad, which will leave everyone hankering for seconds. If the White Rabbit ever catches on, he'll never be late for dinner again.

**" BY THE WAY, I HAVE A FEW MORE HELPFUL HINTS. ONE SIDE MAKES YOU GROW TALLER . . ."
"ONE SIDE OF WHAT . . . ?" "AND THE OTHER SIDE MAKES YOU GROW SHORTER."
"THE OTHER SIDE OF WHAT . . . ?"
"THE MUSHROOM, OF COURSE! "**

HOW TO MAKE IT

4 Servings

45 Preparation Time (minutes)

INGREDIENTS

4 oz.	crimini mushrooms
4 oz.	white mushrooms, small, whole
4 oz.	oyster mushrooms, whole
1 medium	portobello mushroom
1 clove	garlic, chopped
1 tsp.	salt
3 tbs.	olive oil
1 tsp.	chopped thyme
4 tbs.	chopped Italian parsley
12 oz.	spinach
2	plum tomatoes, seeded and diced
3 tbs.	balsamic vinegar
1/4 package	edible flowers (12 blossoms)

➡ Preheat oven to 400°F. Wipe all mushrooms with a damp dish towel.

➡ Quarter the crimini mushrooms.

➡ Remove stem from the portobello mushroom and, with a teaspoon, scrape away gills. Then dice into approximately 1-inch cubes.

➡ In a bowl, mix all mushrooms with garlic, salt, olive oil, and thyme.

➡ Place on a baking sheet, and roast in preheated oven for about 15 minutes, or until mushrooms appear slightly browned around the edges and begin to smell good. Remove from oven and allow to cool.

➡ Toss parsley, spinach, and diced tomatoes with balsamic vinegar, and divide among 4 plates.

➡ Spoon warm mushrooms over each and garnish with edible flowers (3 blossoms per plate). Serve just as spinach begins to wilt.

NUTRITION INFORMATION

Each Serving Contains

Calories	126
Total fat	11 g
Saturated fat	2 g
Sodium	567 mg
Carbohydrates	7 g
Fiber	2 g
Protein	3 g

NOTES

Any combination of mushrooms works well together, just remember to vary colors and sizes. If edible flowers are not available, substitute toasted sunflower seeds.

VARIATIONS

Puree mushrooms in a blender for a wonderful soup or sauce, omitting spinach, plum tomatoes, balsamic vinegar, and edible flowers.

SERVING SUGGESTIONS

Forgo the spinach and this becomes a side dish, or may be eaten with pasta.

MENU IDEAS

This hearty dish full of autumnal flavors is best served before a potent entrée such as roast beef or lamb.

WHAT CHILDREN CAN DO

Little hands can wash and dry the spinach, pluck thyme leaves from stems, and, most important of all, decorate the plates with edible flowers before serving.

The Cheshire Cat's

from Alice in Wonderland

MARINATED FISH SALAD

his dish is as bizarre as the Cheshire Cat: not cooked, not raw, pink and orange marinated fish is indeed a paradox, almost like the pudgy cat himself. The dazzling smile blithely pasted on your face as you down this splendid snack might be a sign of madness, but fear not—it's just what we call "taste gratification." Portions are small enough to entice, yet not big enough to fill, kind of like the Cheshire Cat's last words to Alice: "You may have noticed that I'm not all here myself." One more thing: pay no attention to the friendly, purple-striped cat if he tells you you're bound to lose your way. Follow my instructions and you're sure to be heading in the right direction.

66 CAN YOU STAND ON YOUR HEAD? 99

HOW TO MAKE IT

4 Servings

4 Preparation Time (hours)

INGREDIENTS

4 oz.	beet, juiced
2 tbs.	white vinegar
2 tbs.	water
$^3/_4$ tsp.	salt
$^1/_2$	jalapeño pepper, pureed
$^1/_2$ lb. (2 pieces)	sole fillets
$^1/_2$ cup	lime juice
2 tbs.	chopped cilantro
$^1/_2$ lb.	salmon fillet, tail portion, butterflied
$^1/_2$ head	frisée lettuce
2	Roma tomatoes, seeded, diced
1	shallot, finely diced
$^1/_4$ cup	extra-virgin olive oil
	sea salt, to taste
	black pepper, to taste

➡ Combine beet juice, vinegar, water, $^1/_4$ teaspoon of salt, and pureed jalapeño pepper. Place in a shallow glass bowl large enough so fish may be laid out in one layer.

➡ Cut sole in half from side to side so that there are 2 pieces per fillet in triangular shapes, similar to salmon. Then cut in half lengthwise for a total of 4 pieces.

➡ Place in one layer in beet marinade, dipping to coat both sides. Wrap in plastic and refrigerate for 2 to 3 hours, no more. Thoroughly combine lime juice, $^1/_2$ teaspoon of salt, and cilantro in a similar-sized glass dish.

➡ Butterfly salmon into 2 pieces, about the same thickness; then cut again along spine line, so that the 4 pieces resemble the cuts of sole.

➡ Place in one layer in lime juice marinade, dipping to coat both sides. Wrap with plastic and refrigerate for 2 to 3 hours, no more.

➡ When ready to serve, dry fish fillets on paper towels and divide among 4 plates.

➡ Garnish with frisée lettuce, diced tomatoes, and shallots. Drizzle with olive oil, sea salt, and black pepper to taste.

NUTRITION INFORMATION

Each Serving Contains

Calories	266
Total fat	17 g
Saturated fat	2 g
Sodium	489 mg
Carbohydrates	9 g
Fiber	1 g
Protein	21 g

NOTES

Only saltwater fish fillets work for this recipe. Do not substitute freshwater fish.

SERVING SUGGESTIONS

Double this dish for a light luncheon entrée in the summer, or use smaller portions of fish on endive spears as canapés for a party.

WHAT CHILDREN CAN DO

Kids can help arrange fish on plates and count to make sure everyone gets the same amount.

NOTES

This will feed 2 "bears," or about 4 regular human beings.

VARIATIONS

You can alternate different sliced meats and cheeses in building this sandwich.

SERVING
SUGGESTIONS

This sandwich is best served in the great outdoors, while you're enjoying nature.

MENU IDEAS

Serve with "Horace Horsecollar's Cool Pasta with Salsa Fresca."

WHAT CHILDREN
CAN DO

Kids can help build the sandwich from the bottom up.

Humphrey the Bear's

SANDWICH

from Cartoons

2 Servings

30 Preparation Time (minutes)

INGREDIENTS

1 loaf	Italian bread, 1 foot long
1/4 cup	extra-virgin olive oil
4 leaves	lettuce, shredded
2 oz.	ham, thinly sliced
2 oz.	Swiss cheese, thinly sliced
2	dill pickles, thinly sliced
2 oz.	turkey breast, thinly sliced
3	tomatoes, thinly sliced
2 oz.	roast beef, thinly sliced
2 oz.	Dijon mustard
2 oz.	cheddar cheese, thinly sliced

lice Italian bread lengthwise, remove most of the soft interior, and set aside for bread crumbs.

➡ Drizzle inside sections of bread with olive oil; then begin layering meats, cheeses, and vegetables in the order listed. Top off with the remaining section of bread.

➡ Use long toothpicks to hold the sandwich together; then wrap well in plastic or aluminum foil. Refrigerate 1 to 2 hours before setting off on your picnic.

➡ To serve, use a serrated knife to cut into 4 or more portions.

" **PUT IT IN THE BAG, BUMP! BUMP!** "

NUTRITION INFORMATION

Each Serving Contains

Calories	632
Total fat	36 g
Saturated fat	9 g
Sodium	1,618 mg
Carbohydrates	66 g
Fiber	8 g
Protein	22 g

Bambi and Thumper's GREEN GODDESS DRESSING

from Bambi

4 Servings

1 Preparation Time (hours)

INGREDIENTS

1 cup	mayonnaise
4 tbs.	chopped parsley
³/₄ bunch	scallions, thinly sliced
¹/₄ cup	sour cream
¹/₄ cup	lemon juice
2 tbs.	chopped tarragon
1 tsp.	anchovy paste
1 tsp.	Dijon mustard
¹/₈ tsp.	black pepper to taste

Combine all ingredients in a blender and process until smooth and creamy.

➡ Refrigerate at least 1 hour before serving. If dressing is too thick, thin down with a bit of milk.

❝ EATING GREENS IS A SPECIAL TREAT. . . . IT MAKES LONG EARS . . . AND GREAT BIG FEET! ❞

NOTES

Do not serve this dressing with baby greens—the flavors don't match and this dressing is too heavy for that type of lettuce.

MENU IDEAS

This dressing is great over wedges of iceberg lettuce, garnished with cherry tomatoes and thinly sliced red onions.

NUTRITION INFORMATION

Each Serving Contains

Calories	452
Total fat	47 g
Saturated fat	8 g
Sodium	372 mg
Carbohydrates	7 g
Fiber	1 g
Protein	2 g

Lilo & Stitch's

from Lilo & Stitch

HAWAIIAN SANDWICH

Traveling from outer space to Hawaii is sure to drain anyone of energy, and our little fur ball Stitch has worked up an appetite as big as the waves of the Hawaiian surf. What better way to placate his hunger than with a traditional, yet upbeat American favorite, the sandwich? This "hunka hunka burning love" also helps solidify a "new" family bond between Lilo and her sister, Nani, and of course, Stitch himself. Who would have thought that an experimental alien Elvis fan, found in a Hawaiian dog pound, could change people's views of family relationships?

" 'OHANA' MEANS 'FAMILY'. "

HOW TO MAKE IT

4 Servings

45 Preparation Time (minutes)

INGREDIENTS

¼	pineapple, peeled, thinly sliced
4 oz.	cream cheese, softened
¼ cup	macadamia nuts, crushed
2 tbs.	mayonnaise
4 slices	white bread
4 leaves	green leaf lettuce
8 oz.	ham, sliced
4 slices	whole-wheat bread

NUTRITION INFORMATION

Each Serving Contains

Calories	943
Total fat	27 g
Saturated fat	9 g
Sodium	1,205 mg
Carbohydrates	138 g
Fiber	14 g
Protein	39 g

➡ Heat nonstick pan. Cook pineapple slices until caramelized well on each side. Remove and allow to cool to room temperature.

➡ Combine cream cheese and macadamia nuts. Spread mayonnaise on white bread. Place lettuce and a slice of caramelized pineapple on top.

➡ Divide ham evenly among 4 slices of white bread.

➡ Spread cream cheese mixture on whole-wheat bread.

➡ Top with whole-wheat bread and slice sandwiches diagonally.

NOTES
Served on small rolls, this is great finger food for kids' birthday parties.

SERVING SUGGESTIONS
Serve with "Rafiki's Coconut Drink" for a relaxing afternoon in the sun.

MENU IDEAS
Make this dish part of a beach picnic. Also load your cooler with raw vegetables and ranch dressing, a container of sweet-and-sour three-bean salad, and lots of chocolate-chip cookies.

WHAT CHILDREN CAN DO
Kids can soften cream cheese in a metal mixing bowl with a fork, and crush macadamia nuts.

Melody Time's

COLD POACHED SHRIMP WITH MELONS

*I*n the Melody Time *episode "Blame it on the Samba" (1948), Donald and Joe Carioca meet up with Aracuan Bird, an old buddy of theirs from the adventure-packed* Three Caballeros, *at Café do Samba, where the wacky winged fellow is waiting tables. To lift his friends' spirits, he prepares a crazy cocktail, mixing strange colored liquids beneath a flash of dazzling lights to the wild samba beat. What a night! From Aracuan's menu, we've selected a multicolor salad that's sweet and spicy, subtle and bold, just like the entertainment we're treated to in the movie. A perfect summer dish, when you're hungry for something cool and fulfilling, with a little heat in the background to keep things interesting.*

HOW TO MAKE IT

4 Servings

3 Preparation Time (hours)

INGREDIENTS

¹⁄₄	honeydew melon
¹⁄₄	cantaloupe melon
1 quart	water
2	bay leaves
¹⁄₄ tsp.	dried thyme
1 lb.	shrimp, peeled and deveined
1	lemon, juice and zest
6 tbs.	extra-virgin olive oil
1 tsp.	white-wine vinegar
3 tbs.	green peppercorns, drained and crushed
	salt and pepper to taste
1 tb.	chopped parsley

NUTRITION INFORMATION

Each Serving Contains

Calories	340
Total fat	23 g
Saturated fat	2 g
Sodium	188 mg
Carbohydrates	13 g
Fiber	1 g
Protein	24 g

➡ Peel melons and remove seeds. Slice each melon into 8 equal pieces, and refrigerate.

➡ Bring water to a boil, with bay leaves and thyme. Add shrimp, and simmer for 5 minutes, or until it turns pink. Remove shrimp from water and allow to cool. Prepare dressing while shrimp is cooling.

➡ Mix lemon zest and juice with extra-virgin olive oil, vinegar, peppercorns, and salt and pepper to taste. It should be lemony, while the green peppercorns provide sharpness. Add more of either to your taste.

➡ Cut shrimp in half from tail to top to give a "double" appearance, place in a small glass dish, and pour dressing over all. Marinate for 10 to 15 minutes.

➡ When ready to serve, alternate green and orange melons on a plate; then place marinated shrimp over melon.

➡ Garnish with chopped parsley and pour any extra dressing around—not on—the melon.

NOTES
A solid white fish fillet, such as halibut, grouper, or tilapia, may be used in place of shrimp.

SERVING SUGGESTIONS
Best served on a dark plate for greatest visual appeal.

MENU IDEAS
In the summertime, double the portions for a simple dinner entrée. Or follow this light and fresh dish with a sophisticated yet easy-to-make entrée like "Esmeralda's Turkey Piccata."

WHAT CHILDREN CAN DO

Kids can help assemble shrimp and melon slices for an appealing presentation.

Mowgli's
MIXED VEGETABLE SALAD

hanks to the teachings of his wise and entertaining mentors, Bagheera and Baloo, Mowgli learns to survive deep in the heart of the Indian rain forest. This lovable threesome is probably as mismatched a crew as you'll ever meet, yet it's one for all and all for one, especially in the face of danger. Indeed, their individuality within a cohesive group situation has provided the inspiration for this dish, which blends typically Indian ingredients and spices, harmoniously amalgamating a barrage of different taste sensations. Each vegetable retains its own inherent flavor and texture, first cooked separately then amicably combined.

" CAN I DO IT, TOO?"
"SURE. JUST DO WHAT I DO!"

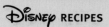

HOW TO MAKE IT

4 Servings

1½ Preparation Time (hours)

INGREDIENTS

2	bananas, green, unripe
½ cup	olive oil
½ tsp.	ground cumin
1 large	onion, peeled, in ½-inch dice
½ tsp.	ground ginger
1 large	yam, peeled, in ½-inch dice
6 oz.	baby yellow pattypan squash, trimmed
½ tsp.	curry powder
¼ lb.	baby spinach
	salt and pepper to taste
2 oz.	peanuts
1	lemon, quartered

→ Preheat oven to 425°F. Peel and cut bananas into 1-inch cubes. Toss them with 1 tablespoon of oil, then place on a baking sheet. In the same bowl, toss ground cumin with 1 tablespoon of oil and bathe pieces of onion, which are then placed on other side of sheet.

→ In another bowl, combine 1 tablespoon of oil and ginger. Toss in pieces of yam, placing on a second baking sheet.

→ In another bowl, toss squash with 1 tablespoon of oil and curry powder. Place on other side of second baking sheet.

→ Place both pans in preheated oven, and bake until veggies become caramelized around the edges, about 20 to 25 minutes. Bananas may cook more quickly. If so, carefully remove with a spatula and place in large mixing bowl.

→ Meanwhile, place washed and dried spinach in large mixing bowl, which will hold all the produce as it comes out of the oven. Place cooked produce on top of the spinach; toss gently. The heat from the produce will be enough to wilt spinach properly. Add salt to taste.

→ Serve warm or at room temperature, but not cold, garnished with peanuts and lemon wedges.

MENU IDEAS

This is perfect for a vegetarian meal with steamed rice and "Kuzco's Spinach Puffs."

WHAT CHILDREN CAN DO

Kids can wash and dry spinach, as they try to name the many animals found in the jungles of India. They can also help arrange cooked veggies in a large serving bowl.

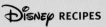
DISNEP RECIPES 125

The Walrus and Carpenter's

from Alice
in Wonderland

FRESH OYSTER SALAD

"Oh, yes, uh, the time has come, my little friends, to talk of food and things," says the Walrus. The Carpenter replies: "Of peppercorn and mustard seed and other seasonings. We'll mix them all together in a sauce that's fit for kings." With such a dressing, oysters become heavenly. As they're small and succulent, briny and sweet, redolent of the sea, there's no wonder why Walrus couldn't keep himself from eating so many. Here, then, is the recipe—as always, simple yet refined. Though the temptation may be great, don't be a walrus when you serve these tasty tidbits: remember to share and share alike.

"THE TIME HAS COME," THE WALRUS SAID,
"TO TALK OF MANY THINGS:
OF SHOES—AND SHIPS—AND SEALING-WAX—
OF CABBAGES—AND KINGS—AND WHY THE SEA
IS BOILING HOT—
AND WHETHER PIGS HAVE
WINGS."

HOW TO MAKE IT

4 Servings

30 Preparation Time (minutes)

INGREDIENTS

¼ tsp.	peppercorns, crushed
½ tsp.	mustard seeds
3	shallots, thinly sliced
2 oz.	Champagne vinegar
⅛ tsp.	sea salt
¼ tsp.	sugar
½ tsp.	chopped thyme
1½	lemons
1 oz.	sweet butter, room temperature
4 slices	pumpernickel bread, toasted
24	oysters, shucked
4 leaves	purple cabbage

➡ Combine crushed peppercorns, mustard seeds, shallots, vinegar, salt, sugar, and thyme. Grate ½ lemon rind into mixture, and squeeze in juice.

➡ Spread butter on cooled pumpernickel toast. Cut off crusts and design attractive shapes— triangles, rectangles, etc.

➡ Open and wash oysters. Replace them on the deep part of the shell, garnishing each one with some sauce.

➡ Serve on plates lined with purple cabbage leaves and an additional wedge of lemon in the center. Serve buttered pumpernickel toast.

NUTRITION INFORMATION

Each Serving Contains

Calories	387
Total fat	10 g
Saturated fat	5 g
Sodium	659 mg
Carbohydrates	66 g
Fiber	2 g
Protein	19 g

NOTES

If you prefer not to serve oysters raw, you can steam them and chill them, using the same sauce.

VARIATIONS

This sauce works equally well with cherrystone clams and steamed mussels.

WHAT CHILDREN CAN DO

Shells may be washed and become part of an arts-and-crafts project on oceanography.

Tinker Bell's

GOLDEN HERB MELANGE

his blend of herbaceous leaves is as varied as Tinker Bell's moods, and as light as her flights of fancy, and comes lightly sprinkled with the capricious fairy's magical "pixie dust." The combination of ingredients here may strike you as slightly bizarre, but this is a foolproof salad that never disappoints. Of course, Tinker Bell uses her powers on a very select few, so use this recipe to bestow a little magic on your favorite people. After a taste of this, you and your guests just might start flying off to Never Land.

" WHAT'S THE PIXIE DOING?"

"TALKING."

"WHAT DID SHE SAY?"

"SHE SAYS YOU'RE A BIG, UGLY GIRL!"

"OH! WELL, I THINK SHE'S LOVELY! "

HOW TO MAKE IT

8 Servings

30 Preparation Time (minutes)

INGREDIENTS

1 bunch	Italian flat leaf parsley
1 bunch	tarragon, leaves only
1 bunch	arugula, leaves only
1 bunch	basil, leaves only
1/2 bunch	thyme, leaves only
1 bunch	chervil, leaves only
1/2 bunch	mint, leaves only
1 head	butter lettuce, whole leaves only
1 oz.	extra-virgin olive oil
1/2 tsp.	sea salt
1	lemon, grated rind only
1/2	orange, grated rind only
2 pieces	edible gold
1/2 package	edible flowers (24 to 32 blossoms)

NUTRITION INFORMATION

Each Serving Contains

Calories	69
Total fat	4 g
Saturated fat	1 g
Sodium	172 mg
Carbohydrates	8 g
Fiber	2 g
Protein	3 g

➡ In a bowl, combine all leaves except butter lettuce.

➡ Garnish 4 small plates with butter lettuce leaves.

➡ Toss herbs with olive oil to coat, add salt, and divide among the 4 garnished plates.

➡ Sprinkle lemon and orange rind over salads, followed by edible gold, and topped off with edible flowers.

NOTES

Edible gold is available at specialty gourmet shops and fine bakeries; it is an optional item that does, however, provide stunning visual impact.

VARIATIONS

Other herbs may be substituted for those listed here, such as watercress, fennel tops, sorrel, and dill.

SERVING SUGGESTIONS

Present this dish on either glass plates or solid white plates for the best visual impact.

MENU IDEAS

A light salad for a fancy party, perhaps preceding a plate of "Uncle Scrooge's Golden Risotto" and followed by "Simba's Seared Fillet of Beef." For dessert, try a slice of "Fauna's Birthday Cake."

Willie the Giant's
MIXED SANDWICH

from Fun and Fancy Free

**SERVING
SUGGESTIONS**

Make sure to have a very
large napkin on hand.

MENU IDEAS

Roast beef may be
substituted for prosciutto,
cheddar cheese may be used
instead of Emmenthal, and
mustard can take the place of
mayonnaise.

**WHAT
CHILDREN CAN DO**

Kids can help assemble
the sandwich, deciding
which ingredient should
go next and spreading
mayonnaise on the bread.

Assemble the sandwich as follows. Spread the 2 slices of bread with mayonnaise. On one, place sliced roasted turkey, Emmenthal cheese, some of the pickled onions (sliced for easy eating), and top it off with green lettuce and prosciutto.

➡ Pop on the second slice of bread and, for civilized snackers, cut the sandwich in half before serving (ogres, giants, and other brutes can grab their sandwiches whole and munch away without worrying about crumbs in their beards or stains on their shirts).

1	Servings
15	Preparation Time (minutes)

INGREDIENTS

2 slices	white bread
1/4 cup	mayonnaise
4 oz.	roast turkey leg, sliced
2 oz.	Emmenthal cheese, sliced
2 oz.	onions, pickled, halved*
2 pieces	green leaf lettuce
1 oz.	prosciutto, sliced
	freshly ground black pepper to taste

*Available at specialty food stores

NUTRITION INFORMATION
Each Serving Contains

Calories	1,085
Total fat	71 g
Saturated fat	20 g
Sodium	1,860 mg
Carbohydrates	52 g
Fiber	16 g
Protein	63 g

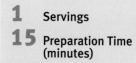

" SAY, HAS ANYONE SEEN ANY SIGNS OF A TEENSY-WEENSY LITTLE MOUSE? "

Vegetables and Vegetarian Entrées

Mrs. Price's

from Bedknobs and Broomsticks

CABBAGE BUDS WITH BRAISED NETTLES

o you know Mrs. Eglantine Price? She is an "amateur witch" who keeps in shape thanks to her own very special and healthy diet of cabbage buds, rose hips, glyssop seed, elm bark, whortle yeast, and stewed nettles. Indeed, as she warns her three young guests, Carrie, Paul, and Charlie: "I'm afraid I don't know much about what children eat. You'll have to make do as I do." So here, straight from her book of "spells," is a nutritious vegetarian dish. Also, try her famous Mango Wuzzle Jam, page 134, great on breakfast toast or as a garnish for a steamy bowl of oatmeal on cold mornings.

66 I'M AFRAID YOU WON'T FIND ANY FRIED FOODS IN THIS HOUSE. 99

HOW TO MAKE IT

4 Servings

30 Preparation Time (minutes)

INGREDIENTS

1 quart	water
1 lb.	brussels sprouts, cleaned
8 oz.	nettles, cleaned well
$1/4$ tsp.	salt
2 tbs.	extra-virgin olive oil
2 tsps.	mustard seeds
	pepper, to taste

NUTRITION INFORMATION

Each Serving Contains

Calories	124
Total fat	8 g
Saturated fat	1 g
Sodium	198 mg
Carbohydrates	11 g
Fiber	6 g
Protein	5 g

➜ In a pot, bring water to boiling.

➜ Trim cleaned brussels sprouts and cut an *X* in the bottom of each stem; set aside until water boils.

➜ Carefully trim nettle leaves from stems (wear gloves to avoid being stung by the prickly tendrils on the stalks), wash leaves, and set aside.

➜ Add $1/4$ teaspoon salt and brussels sprouts to boiling water, return to a boil, and cook until crisp yet tender, about 5 minutes.

➜ Heat olive oil in a nonstick pan; sauté mustard seeds until they begin to pop.

➜ Add cleaned nettles and quickly cover with a lid to prevent spattering. When popping sound stops, remove cover and sauté until greens are wilted.

➜ Drain cooked brussels sprouts and add to braising nettles; cook for an additional 1 minute or so.

➜ Season with salt and pepper, to taste.

NOTES
If nettles aren't available, use young spinach leaves.

MENU IDEAS
A fine accompaniment to this healthy fare would be a serving of "Peg Leg Pete's Seared Swordfish with Minted Bread-Crumb Sauce."

VARIATIONS
Cook each vegetable separately; serve brussels sprouts inside a ring of sautéed nettles.

WHAT CHILDREN CAN DO
Kids can clean brussels sprouts and, with proper supervision, cut a tiny *X* in the bottom of each. They can also wash spinach leaves when nettles are not available.

VARIATIONS
This jam may also be made
with peaches.

BEVERAGE
SUGGESTIONS
This dish is best accompanied
by sparkling mineral water.

HOW TO MAKE IT

MANGO WUZZLE JAM

➡ Peel mangoes, remove seeds, and cut in cubes; then place
in a large heavy pot along with lime juice and water over
high heat. Bring to a rolling boil, stirring constantly.

➡ Add sugar and cardamom seeds. Return to a rolling boil;
cook for 15 to 20 minutes.

➡ Add candied ginger, boil for an additional 3-4 minutes.
Remove from heat, skim off foam, and ladle hot jam into
clean containers.

➡ Refrigerate until ready to serve. May be stored in
refrigerator for up to two months.

8	Servings
2	Preparation Time (hours)

INGREDIENTS

6 lbs.	mangoes
2 oz.	lime juice
2 cups	water
24 oz.	sugar
$1/4$ tsp.	cardamom seeds, outer covering removed
2 oz.	candied gingerroot, finely diced

**❝ AND IN THE POT THERE,
MANGO WUZZLE JAM!❞
❝MANGO WUZZLE?❞
❝YES, VERY NOURISHING! ❞**

Peter Pan's
CRISPY SPINACH WITH "PIXIE DUST"

from Peter Pan

4 Servings

45 Preparation Time (minutes)

INGREDIENTS

12 oz.	spinach leaves, washed and dried
1/3 tsp.	salt
	freshly ground pepper, to taste
1 tsp.	grated lemon zest
1 tsp.	grated orange zest
4 leaves	edible gold (optional)
as needed	olive oil, for deep frying

NUTRITION INFORMATION

Each Serving Contains

Calories	76
Total fat	7 g
Saturated fat	1 g
Sodium	226 mg
Carbohydrates	2 g
Fiber	2 g
Protein	2 g

emove stems from washed spinach, and dry thoroughly.

➡ Heat oil to 350°F in a deep pot or electric fryer. Fry spinach in small batches until crispy. While cooking, it will go limp briefly; then, as the water evaporates, the leaves will turn crispy—don't worry. Remove when desired crispiness is reached, and place fried leaves on a paper towel–lined cookie sheet.

➡ Divide evenly among four plates, sprinkling on salt, pepper, and lemon and orange zests. Sprinkle the edible gold leaf on top of each leaf, so as to resemble "pixie dust."

> **❝ ALL IT TAKES IS FAITH AND TRUST. . . OH! AND SOMETHING I FORGOT: DUST!" "DUST?" " YUP, JUST A LITTLE BIT OF PIXIE DUST! ❞**

NOTES
You may prepare fried spinach a few hours in advance only on a NONHUMID day—otherwise, crispy spinach will become soggy due to the humidity in the air.

SERVING SUGGESTIONS
This is a spectacular dish, best served on plain white plates for visual impact (dark-colored plates decrease visibility).

MENU IDEAS
This dish would be great served before "Melody Time's Cold Poached Shrimp with Melons," followed by a piece of "Huey, Dewey, and Louie's Chocolate Pie."

Fun and Fancy Free's
RATATOUILLE

from Fun and Fancy Free

*I*n the 1947 movie Fun and Fancy Free, *Jiminy Cricket, Bongo, Goofy, the Singing Harp, Mickey, Donald, and of course, Willie the Giant begin by developing their own personalities, but by the end of the show they come together to form a solid, unified group, thanks to the imagination of a kindly storyteller played by ventriloquist Edgar Bergen. As with story development and plot lines, recipe development is not much different. Each vegetable here was chosen and is cooked separately to bring out its best flavor/color/texture, then combined near the end to produce a unified, tasty, eye-catching composition, just like the plot of* Fun and Fancy Free.

❝ THEN THERE CAME THE EVENING WHEN MICKEY, DONALD, AND GOOFY SAT DOWN TO DINNER AND ALL THAT REMAINED WAS A SINGLE BEAN TO SPLIT THREE WAYS. . . ❞

HOW TO MAKE IT

4 Servings

2 Preparation Time (hours)

INGREDIENTS

6 tbs.	extra-virgin olive oil
2 small	onions, 1½-inch cube
2 small	zucchini, 1½-inch cube
1	red bell pepper, 1½-inch cube
1	green bell pepper, 1½-inch cube
1 medium	eggplant, 1½-inch cube
2 cloves	garlic, chopped
1 lb.	tomatoes, canned, drained
2 oz.	tomato paste
2 tbs.	chopped parsley
2 tbs.	chopped basil
	salt and pepper, to taste

➡ Preheat oven to 350°F. Place olive oil in large mixing bowl, add onions, and toss well. Remove onions to an oven pan, leaving as much oil in the bowl as possible.

➡ Continue with each vegetable in the same manner, placing each one on a separate oven pan. Once all the vegetables have been oiled and placed in pans, sprinkle lightly with salt and roast for about 15 minutes in preheated oven before checking. Vegetables should be cooked, while still retaining their integrity.

➡ Meanwhile, sauté garlic with remaining olive oil in a saucepan until fragrant but not browned. Add drained tomatoes, breaking up with the back of a spoon, followed by tomato paste, parsley, and basil.

➡ Cook at a medium simmer for about 10 minutes; then toss in cooked vegetables, adding salt and pepper to taste. May be served hot or at room temperature.

NUTRITION INFORMATION

Each Serving Contains

Calories	262
Total fat	19 g
Saturated fat	3 g
Sodium	750 mg
Carbohydrates	23 g
Fiber	7g
Protein	5 g

SERVING SUGGESTIONS

Serve alongside grilled fish or as part of a vegetarian meal.

MENU IDEAS

Try this on your next brunch menu, served with a fried or poached egg on top. It may also be tossed with a large type of pasta, such as penne or farfalle, and served either hot, at room temperature, or chilled.

Kuzco's SPINACH PUFFS

from The Emperor's New Groove

Kronk and Yzma's dinner for Emperor Kuzco is comprised of a truly "delicate" vegetarian menu, including soup, a light salad, steamed broccoli, dessert, and coffee. And oh, yes—how could I forget?—these lovely spinach puffs prepared with surprising care and elegance by the usually absentminded Kronk. They're actually a snap to make and will be a sure hit on any table. These go great with a chilled glass of wine, though avoid cocktails of your own invention—why risk turning your guests into llamas?

**66 OH, THEY'RE SO EASY TO MAKE.
I'LL GET YOU THE RECIPE. 99**

HOW TO MAKE IT

4 Servings

2 Preparation Time (hours)

INGREDIENTS

2 lbs.	spinach, well washed
2 tbs.	extra-virgin olive oil
1 clove	garlic, finely minced
1 tsp.	dried dill
4 oz.	feta cheese, crumbled
$1/8$ tsp.	black pepper
1	egg, beaten
$1/2$ package	phyllo dough, defrosted
4 tbs.	butter, melted

NUTRITION INFORMATION

Each Serving Contains

Calories	297
Total fat	26 g
Saturated fat	12 g
Sodium	588 mg
Carbohydrates	9 g
Fiber	5 g
Protein	11 g

➡ Steam spinach until it wilts, cool in a colander until comfortable enough to handle, then squeeze out as much liquid as possible.

➡ Place spinach on a cutting board and chop finely. Heat olive oil, sauté garlic until fragrant, add spinach and dill, then cook until most of the moisture has evaporated.

➡ When dry, place spinach mixture on a baking sheet, spreading out to cool quickly at room temperature. When cool, add feta cheese, black pepper, and egg, mixing well.

➡ Preheat oven to 350°F. Line cookie sheet with parchment paper for easy cleanup. Carefully remove phyllo dough from package, then cover with a damp dish towel.

➡ With a sharp knife or pizza cutter, cut phyllo dough into long rectangles about 4 inches by 9 inches. Cover again with towels to prevent drying. Divide dough into 8 portions, one rectangle at a time, and brush with melted butter.

➡ Place $1/8$ of the spinach mixture at bottom of each strip. Fold up from bottom to one side to form a triangle; continue folding back and forth to completely encase spinach filling. Place triangle-shaped puffs on prepared cookie sheet and brush again with melted butter.

➡ Puffs may be baked immediately in preheated oven until they turn brown, 15-20 minutes, or frozen for later use. Frozen puffs go directly from freezer to oven, and are baked for 20 to 30 minutes.

VARIATIONS
Make smaller or larger triangles as you prefer, in each case adjusting the amount of filling and cooking time to match desired size.

MENU IDEAS
Start the meal just like Kuzco does, with soup and a light salad, followed by "King Hubert's Veal Roast with Apricots and Thyme" for a hearty and satisfying meal.

SERVING SUGGESTIONS
These little morsels are great to bring along on a picnic. Most folks probably never thought that spinach could taste so good.

WHAT CHILDREN CAN DO
Kids will love folding dough into triangles and "painting" them with butter.

Pocahontas's

from Pocahontas

SAVORY INDIAN CORN PUDDING

I n 1607, Pocahontas and John Smith met in Virginia beneath a cascading waterfall. They came from two very different worlds and spoke different languages, yet they immediately understood each other. We've come up with this recipe in honor of their endearing love story. It's a simple and satisfying creation that combines Native American corn and European cooking techniques, in perfect harmony—just like Pocahontas and John Smith. Perhaps even Flit the hummingbird will help you pick "sun-sweetened" berries for decorations.

"AND LOOK. IT'S FOOD!"

"WHAT IS IT?"

"IT'S BETTER THAN HARDTACK AND GRUEL, THAT'S FOR SURE!"

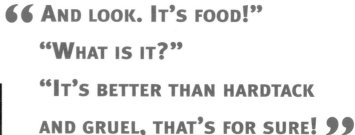

HOW TO MAKE IT

6   Servings

1   Preparation Time (hour)

INGREDIENTS

6 oz.	corn kernels, whole
7 oz.	corn kernels, pureed
$\frac{1}{4}$ tsp.	chopped thyme
$\frac{1}{2}$ tsp.	chopped parsley
2 cups	milk
1 tb.	flour
$\frac{1}{4}$ tsp.	salt
$\frac{1}{8}$ tsp.	white pepper
3	eggs
2	egg whites
1 quart	boiling water
1 tb.	olive oil
4 oz.	blackberries

NUTRITION INFORMATION

Each Serving Contains

Calories	141
Total fat	5 g
Saturated fat	2 g
Sodium	181 mg
Carbohydrates	21 g
Fiber	3 g
Protein	9 g

➡ Combine corn, thyme, parsley, milk, flour, salt, and white pepper in a saucepan. Bring to a boil, remove from heat, and allow to cool completely.

➡ In a separate large bowl, combine eggs and egg whites. Beat well; then allow bubbles to disappear. Eggs and cooled ingredients in saucepan should be ready at the same time for the next step.

➡ Preheat oven to 350°F. Prepare pot of boiling water. Coat 6 individual custard molds with olive oil and place in a 2-inch-deep baking pan.

➡ Combine cooled corn mixture and beaten eggs gently but well. Divide evenly among the individual molds, then pour boiling water around them in order to soften the impact of the heat and add moisture to the oven while cooking.

➡ Place in preheated oven and bake for 15 to 20 minutes, or until firmly set and only slightly "shaky" in the middle.

➡ Garnish with sun-sweetened blackberries for an authentic taste sensation.

NOTES

While canned or frozen corn works for this dish, fresh corn is sweeter and more tender.

VARIATIONS

Whole corn kernels may be roasted for a sweeter, smokier flavor.

MENU IDEAS

Served alongside "Captain Hook's Codfish Fillet," this will make a dish that is not only colorful but healthy and tasty as well.

WHAT CHILDREN CAN DO

Little ones can help to beat the egg yolks and egg whites as well as inspecting the berries for cleanliness before they are cooked.

Uncle Scrooge's

GOLDEN RISOTTO

*G*old and more gold! Look at it, touch it, and if you can't get enough of it, try eating it! Gold is Uncle Scrooge's main preoccupation, as he counts and recounts his vast fortune, more than "three acres of money" to be exact. Beholding a dish of this golden yellow risotto, we're sure the old miser's eyes would sparkle with joy. The dish blended with saffron, the spice worth its weight in gold, and served with a crowning touch of edible gold on top. The soft, warm glow this elegant dish provides is proof of your great generosity toward friends and family, a sign of how much you care.

> **" AND I LIKE TO DIVE AROUND MY MONEY LIKE A PORPOISE. . . "**

HOW TO MAKE IT

4 Servings

1 Preparation Time (hour)

INGREDIENTS

6 cups	low-salt vegetable broth
1/2 tsp.	saffron threads
2 tbs.	unsalted butter
2 tbs.	extra-virgin olive oil
1 medium	onion, finely diced
1 lb.	Arborio rice
1/2 cup	dry white wine
3 oz.	Parmesan cheese, freshly grated
1 piece	edible gold*
	salt and pepper, to taste

* Edible gold is available in specialty gourmet shops and fine bakeries.

NUTRITION INFORMATION

Each Serving Contains

Calories	822
Total fat	28 g
Saturated fat	12 g
Sodium	1,405 mg
Carbohydrates	116 g
Fiber	7 g
Protein	21 g

➡ Bring vegetable broth and saffron to a boil; then reduce to a simmer and proceed to the next step.

➡ Melt 1 ounce of butter and olive oil in a pan. When butter begins to sizzle, add onion and sauté until translucent.

➡ Add rice and sauté until coated and somewhat translucent, about 5 to 6 minutes. Slowly add wine. Stir in a single direction until most of the wine has evaporated.

➡ Add a ladleful of stock. Continue to stir in the same direction until incorporated. Do not add more stock until the previous amount has been completely absorbed. Continue until all the stock has been used and/or the rice is al dente, about 15 to 20 minutes from the start.

➡ Remove pot from heat and add final ounce of butter and Parmesan cheese. Shred the "gold" over the top just before serving.

MENU IDEAS

You might preface this dish with a salad with "Bambi and Thumper's Green Goddess Dressing" and follow up with "Esmeralda's Turkey Piccata."

VARIATIONS

Add fresh peas or quickly sautéed asparagus tips to your risotto just prior to serving, for additional texture, flavor, and visual appeal.

SERVING SUGGESTIONS

Refrigerate leftover risotto in a flat plate or pan. The next day, cut into shapes and sauté in olive oil. Serve in any number of ways: alone as a quick appetizer, as an entrée with a light stew poured over the top, or simply alongside fried eggs for a rich, extra special breakfast.

WHAT CHILDREN CAN DO

With parental supervision kids can help stir the risotto or, using safety scissors, they can help cut the "gold" foil into little strips to decorate the top of the risotto before it is served.

Three Caballeros' VEGETARIAN BURRITOS

from The Three Caballeros

*I*n the famed movie The Three Caballeros *(1945)*, Donald Duck heads south of the border to sunny Mexico with pals José Carioca and Panchito. Wearing their enormous sombreros, the three lovable "amigos" take off on a magical "flying serape" to discover the traditions and customs of this extraordinary land—with lots of snappy local music in the background. As the wacky threesome's euphoria tends to be contagious, perhaps you'd like to undertake a Mexican exploration of your own. The traditional burrito is as colorful and spicy as Donald and his friends— perhaps a little too spicy for some, in which case all you need to do is cut down on the amount of jalapeño pepper used.

**❝ HERE, AMIGOS.
DONALD! JOSE!
HA, HA, HA!
CARAMBA!
NOW WE ARE
THREE CABALLEROS!
YAAAA! ❞**

HOW TO MAKE IT

4 Servings

1¼ Preparation Time (hours)

INGREDIENTS

SALSA

6 small	Roma tomatoes, seeded, finely diced
½ small	onion, finely chopped
1	jalapeño, finely diced
2 tbs.	chopped cilantro
½ tsp.	salt

GUACAMOLE

1	avocado, peeled, seeded, mashed
	juice of ½ lime
¼ tsp.	salt
½ small	onion, finely diced
1 small	Roma tomato, seeded and diced

NUTRITION INFORMATION

Each Serving Contains

Calories	745
Total fat	29 g
Saturated fat	8 g
Sodium	910 mg
Carbohydrates	119 g
Fiber	34 g
Protein	36 g

SALSA

➡ Finely dice tomatoes and add to chopped onion, jalapeño, cilantro, and salt. Refrigerate until needed.

GUACAMOLE

➡ Combine avocado, lime juice, salt, diced onion, and tomato. Refrigerate until needed.

MENU IDEAS

Serve burritos with chips and salsa, cups of "Saludos Amigos' Gazpacho," and slices of watermelon for dessert.

SERVING SUGGESTIONS

Wrap burritos in foil, the way they're served at any favorite taqueria, and enjoy them outside on a nice day. Also, try some sodas imported from Mexico for a different taste treat.

VARIATIONS
Feel free to use different sautéed mixed vegetables and different varieties of beans. For those of you who desire maximum heat, use canned chipotle chilies in adobo, but be sure to have a fire extinguisher ready!

HOW TO MAKE IT

BURRITO FILLING

➡ Heat 1 teaspoon olive oil in a nonstick pan, and sauté garlic until fragrant, 1-2 minutes. Mash cooked pinto beans, then add to sautéing garlic, continuing to mash with a wooden spoon. Cook for several minutes, then remove and keep warm.

➡ Combine cooked white rice, chopped cilantro, lime juice, and finely diced jalapeño, and keep warm. In a nonstick pan, heat remaining amount of olive oil, and sauté both bell peppers and onion on high heat until just wilted.

ASSEMBLY

➡ Heat flour tortillas in a microwave under a damp tea towel until hot, 1-2 minutes. Place tortillas on work surface and divide rice mixture among them, placing it at bottom third of each tortilla.

➡ Next add refried beans, then the sautéed vegetables. Sprinkle with Cheddar cheese and begin rolling up from the bottom; then fold in the sides and place on plate, seam side down.

➡ Return to microwave for about 1 minute to melt cheese. Top with sour cream, guacamole, and salsa.

BURRITOS	
1/4 cup	olive oil
1/2 clove	garlic
1 lb.	pinto beans, cooked
6 oz.	cooked white rice
1/4 bunch	cilantro, chopped
	juice of 2 limes
1/2	jalapeño, finely diced
1/2	red bell pepper, julienned
1/2	green bell pepper, julienned
1/2	medium onion, peeled, julienned
4	flour tortillas
2 oz.	cheddar cheese, shredded
2 oz.	sour cream

Pumbaa and Timon's
POTATOES WITH CARAMELIZED ONIONS

from The Lion King

MENU IDEAS
A hearty side dish like this deserves a hearty entrée—perhaps "Pecos Bill's Grilled Rib-Eye Steak with Red-Eye Gravy."

NOTES
Make twice as much and freeze leftovers in the form of patties. They may be sautéed in olive oil directly from the freezer.

VARIATION
Sprinkle oven-toasted pecans on top of the completed dish for a nice variation in texture and added sophistication.

4 Servings

1 Preparation Time (hour)

INGREDIENTS

1½ lbs.	russet potatoes, washed well
½ cup	extra-virgin olive oil
8 oz.	onions, peeled
	salt and pepper, to taste

NUTRITION INFORMATION
Each Serving Contains

Calories	362
Total fat	29 g
Saturated fat	4 g
Sodium	218 mg
Carbohydrates	25 g
Fiber	3 g
Protein	3 g

Preheat oven to 350°F. Place scrubbed potatoes in oven, directly on rack. Bake for about 30 minutes. Meanwhile, heat olive oil in a large nonstick pan.

➡ Dice onions into 1-inch cubes, place in hot oil, and reduce temperature to medium. Continue to cook, uncovered, until they are deeply caramelized, the color of tea. This should also take about 30 minutes.

➡ When potatoes yield a bit, remove from oven and allow to cool. Slice cooled potatoes thickly, add to onion mixture, and toss lightly. Cook, partially covered, until potatoes are done and a bit crispy, 10-12 minutes.

➡ Add a bit more olive oil if potatoes are sticking. Do not move them too much, or you will have potato hash. Season with salt and pepper to taste.

66 THESE ARE RARE DELICACIES.

MMMMM . . . PECANS!

WITH A VERY

PLEASANT

CRUNCH! 99

The Three Little Pigs'

from Three Little Pigs

POTATO PANCAKES WITH APPLESAUCE

hether it's Fifer with his house of straw, Fiddler with his house of sticks, or Practical who built his house of bricks, they all need wholesome nourishment, just like you. After a meal of these savory pancakes, accented with fresh tart apple sauce, you'll be ready to build your own house, and strong enough to perform the feat with one hand tied behind your back. The pancakes are as soft as the straw Fifer used for his home, lightly browned to the color of Fiddler's stick house, and as substantial as Practical's brick dwelling. But eat too many of these treats and you may begin to resemble one of the trio, if not all three.

" OUR JOB WILL BE TO FURNISH YOU WITH MUSIC – WHILE YOU'RE WORKING! "

HOW TO MAKE IT

4 Servings

1 Preparation Time (hours)

INGREDIENTS

4 lbs.	russet potatoes, peeled
8 oz.	onions, peeled
2	eggs, beaten
4 tbs.	flour
2 cups	olive oil
	salt and pepper, to taste

NUTRITION INFORMATION

Each Serving Contains

Calories	1,123
Total fat	99 g
Saturated fat	7 g
Sodium	258 mg
Carbohydrate	70 g
Fiber	6 g
Protein	6 g

➡ Alternately grate potatoes and onions into a large colander with a bowl underneath, and mix well. (The reason you alternate onion and potato is to prevent oxidation of the potato.) Pour off the water in the bowl under the colander, but do not discard the natural potato starch that settles on the bottom of the bowl.

➡ Transfer grated potatoes and onions to bowl, add eggs, flour, salt, and pepper, and mix well.

➡ Heat olive oil to about 350°F. Fry large spoonfuls of batter until golden brown on each side. Remove to a paper towel–lined baking sheet. Keep warm in a preheated 300°F oven until all are done.

➡ Serve hot, with cold applesauce.

VARIATIONS

Different potatoes can be used to achieve different results. A good substitute is Yukon Gold. Sweet potatoes and yams are a tasty alternative. They also will brown much more quickly due to the higher amounts of sugar they contain, and will produce a somewhat soggy cake.

MENU IDEAS

A wonderful accompaniment to these pancakes and apple sauce is "Oliver & Company's Dry-Roasted Chicken" and steamed green beans.

VARIATIONS

Different apples have different flavors. Some prefer a tart apple like a Granny Smith. But feel free to use your own favorite apple, or even substitute with pears.

**SERVING
SUGGESTIONS**

Applesauce is splendid alongside potato pancakes. For a tasty snack or dessert, try a simple bowl of warm apple sauce with a scoop of vanilla ice cream melting in the middle.

**WHAT
CHILDREN CAN DO**

Kids can mash apples after they are cooked.

HOW TO MAKE IT

APPLESAUCE

➡ Combine all ingredients in a saucepan, bring to a boil, then reduce to a simmer, partly covered.

➡ Cook until mixture begins to break down, stirring occasionally and checking the bottom for scorching. If mixture looks dry, add a bit more apple juice. Applesauce is done when it has the texture of lumpy mashed potatoes.

➡ Allow to cool in saucepan for about $1/2$ hour; then remove cinnamon stick. Mash with potato masher if a smoother texture is desired.

➡ Add sugar to taste, though many prefer on the tart side. Applesauce may be made 2-3 days in advance.

4 Servings

45 Preparation Time (minutes)

INGREDIENTS

2 lbs.	tart apples, peeled and wedged
$1/2$ cup	apple juice
1	cinnamon stick, small
2 oz.	sugar

NUTRITION INFORMATION

Each Serving Contains

Calories	195
Total fat	9 g
Saturated fat	2 g
Sodium	2 mg
Carbohydrates	51 g
Fiber	8 g
Protein	1 g

Desserts

The Aristocats'

"CRÈME DE LA CRÈME" WITH MILK AND HONEY

*P*lain and simple appearances often mask the best surprises, and this dish is no exception. A creamy concoction similar to the one Edgar served to Duchess and her kittens— Toulouse, Berlioz, and Marie—it is laced with tasty treats inside and out, not the butler's sleeping pills. It can be easily re-created in your home and will provide dreamy sensations of comfort as you eat your way through. No need for a taste tester like Roquefort, either!

❝ DELICIOUS. DOUBLE DELICIOUS. THIS CALLS FOR ANOTHER CRACKER. ❞

HOW TO MAKE IT

4 Servings

6 Preparation Time (hours)

INGREDIENTS

1 tsp.	powdered gelatin
2 tbs.	cold water
8 oz.	light cream
1 cup	milk
2 oz.	sugar
1 pinch	salt
¾ tsp.	vanilla extract
4 oz.	crème fraîche
2 tbs.	pine nuts, toasted well
1 oz.	honey, lavender variety
2 tbs.	candied violets (optional)
2 oz.	raspberries

NUTRITION INFORMATION

Each Serving Contains

Calories	315
Total fat	22 g
Saturated fat	13 g
Sodium	105 mg
Carbohydrates	23 g
Fiber	1 g
Protein	6 g

➡ Sprinkle gelatin over cold water and let stand for 5 minutes. In a saucepan, warm light cream and milk with sugar, salt, and vanilla, making sure not to boil. Stir in gelatin until thoroughly dissolved. Remove mixture from heat and let cool for about 5 minutes.

➡ Pour crème fraîche into a medium-sized bowl and slowly whisk in warm milk mixture a little at a time until smooth.

➡ Rinse 8 small ramekins or custard cups (about 6 ounces each) with cold water. Pour creamy mixture into each until three-quarters full and garnish with 1 teaspoon of toasted pine nuts. Cover with plastic wrap, and refrigerate overnight.

➡ To serve, dip cups in hot water to loosen; then place a dessert plate on top and quickly flip. After carefully pulling off cup, your dessert should remain intact on the plate.

➡ Warm honey gently, using either the double-boiler method or a microwave.

➡ Garnish with candied violets and raspberries; then drizzle with honey.

NOTES
Other berries may be used for garnish. Maple syrup may be used instead of honey.

SERVING SUGGESTIONS
Serve on a black plate for major visual impact.

MENU IDEAS
A great dessert after a dinner of "Oliver & Company's Dry-Roasted Chicken" and rosemary-roasted potatoes.

WHAT CHILDREN CAN DO
Children can help decorate the finished dishes with candied violets, raspberries, and honey.

The Rescuers'

from The Rescuers *and* The Rescuers Down Under

SWEET POTATO PIE
WITH CHEESE

ianca and Bertrand, two lovable mice from New York, are members of the International Rescue Aid Society and travel the world over on their heroic rescue missions. In The Rescuers Down Under *(1990)*, duty calls right in the middle of their romantic, candlelit dinner in an exclusive restaurant. They have no choice but to skip what must surely have been an exquisite dessert. Here's a chance to make it up to them with this pie of soft pureed sweet potatoes, lightly spiced and served in a simple crust with tiny morsels of sweet cheese (Gjetost) from Norway. Now that's a dish as sophisticated as Miss Bianca and as spirited as Bertrand. Make some for your next romantic interlude—that is, if you don't plan on being called out on a rescue mission.

**❝ BEFORE TAKEOFF: IF AT FIRST YOU DON'T SUCCEED . . .
TRY, TRY, AGAIN! ❞**

HOW TO MAKE IT

6 Servings

3 Preparation Time (hours)

INGREDIENTS

PIECRUST

8 oz.	flour
1 pinch	salt
4 tbs.	unsalted butter
2¹/₂ tbs.	ice water

FILLING

3 lbs.	sweet potatoes, scrubbed well
4 tbs.	butter
1 cup	evaporated milk
12 oz.	sugar
2	eggs
¹/₂ tsp.	nutmeg
1 tsp.	vanilla extract
¹/₈ tsp.	ground cinnamon
4 oz.	Gjetost cheese, finely diced

NUTRITION INFORMATION

Each Serving Contains

Calories	805
Total fat	20 g
Saturated fat	12 g
Sodium	456 mg
Carbohydrates	135 g
Fiber	5 g
Protein	23 g

PIECRUST

➡ Preheat oven to 350°F. Place flour and salt in the bowl of a food processor, and pulse once or twice to combine.

➡ Add butter, and pulse on and off until mixture resembles small peas.

➡ Sprinkle in cold water and pulse 3-4 times until a ball is formed. Remove and shape into a flat disk; then refrigerate for 15 minutes.

➡ When cold, place dough between 2 sheets of waxed paper and roll into a 10-inch circle. Reroll dough onto a rolling pin, then fit it into pie pan, shaping edges attractively. Prick the bottom with a fork and place in preheated oven for 10 to 12 minutes, or until lightly colored. Remove and cool.

FILLING

➡ Place scrubbed potatoes directly on oven rack and roast until soft to the touch, about 1 hour, depending on size of potatoes. Remove from oven when soft, and let potatoes cool enough to handle.

➡ When cool, remove skins and place in a bowl. Mix with handheld mixer on medium until soft and lump free. Stop every so often, as strings build up on the beater— remove them for a smooth filling.

➡ Add butter, evaporated milk, and sugar, continuing to mix.

➡ Add eggs, nutmeg, vanilla, and cinnamon, blending well.

➡ Fold in diced cheese; then place mixture in prebaked crust.

➡ Bake in preheated oven for about 45 minutes or until set— a knife inserted in the center should come out clean. Cool 1 hour before serving.

NOTES

Can be made without Gjetost cheese if unavailable; however, it is worth searching out. It is of Norwegian origin, and has a strong caramel flavor.

SERVING SUGGESTIONS

Try serving this dish with browned sour cream. Simply mix 1 cup of sour cream or crème fraîche with 2 to 3 tablespoons of brown sugar; then allow the mixture to amalgamate for about 1 hour before serving alongside pie.

MENU IDEAS

Serve this dessert after a meal of fried chicken, potato salad, and coleslaw, with lemonade as the beverage of choice.

WHAT CHILDREN CAN DO

Kids can give potatoes an initial mashing with a potato masher. Let them break the eggs as well, and crumble cheese into small pieces with their hands.

Daisy Duck's

ORANGE-FLAVORED BROWNIES

ime and time again Daisy Duck has to put up with her beloved Donald's shenanigans (though on occasion she can be just as fickle), so what better way to sweeten him up a bit than with an exquisite dessert? Lightly sweet without being capricious, this harmonious recipe is surprisingly easy to follow. And while these brownies may be stylish and sophisticated, rest assured that even youngsters will eagerly gobble them up. Make a double batch and freeze some for a special treat when you're in a hurry.

" UNTIL YOU DEVELOP A MORE PLEASANT PERSONALITY, I DON'T WANT TO EVER SEE YOU AGAIN! "

HOW TO MAKE IT

9 Servings

1 Preparation Time (hour)

INGREDIENTS

8 tbs.	unsalted butter, room temperature
8 oz.	sugar
8 tbs.	cocoa powder
1 tsp.	vanilla extract
1 tsp.	grated orange zest
3	eggs, beaten
1/4 cup	water
5 oz.	flour
1/4 tsp.	salt
1/2 tsp.	baking powder

NUTRITION INFORMATION

Each Serving Contains

Calories	193
Total fat	7 g
Saturated fat	4 g
Sodium	100 mg
Carbohydrates	31 g
Protein	18 g
Fiber	1 g

➡ Preheat oven to 350°F.

➡ Grease a 9-inch x 9-inch baking pan well and line bottom with parchment paper (so the brownies are guaranteed to come out of the pan without sticking and breaking).

➡ Melt butter until liquid but not separated (it should look creamy, pale yellow, and smooth); then mix with sugar, cocoa, vanilla, and orange rind, and allow to cool.

➡ Add eggs and water to mixture, blending well.

➡ In a separate bowl, combine flour, salt, and baking powder, and then add to wet mixture.

➡ Pour batter into prepared baking pan and smooth out top; it will be stiff. Bake in preheated oven for approximately 30 minutes, or until an inserted toothpick comes out clean.

➡ Cool in pan for about 15 minutes. Run knife along side of pan to loosen, invert onto a flat tray or plate, then peel off paper and flip carefully so the top is once again on top.

➡ Cool completely before cutting—if not, brownies will crack badly.

SERVING SUGGESTIONS
Great with sliced strawberries poured over the top.

VARIATIONS
Cut brownies into squares and freeze; when firm, split in half. Stuff with softened ice cream and refreeze. When solid, wrap individually for future use—great for barbecues or birthday parties. They can also be made into brownie drop-cookies by dropping teaspoonfuls onto a greased baking sheet—bake for 10 to 12 minutes or until puttylike in consistency. Try the "Rocky Road" style: substitute orange rind with walnuts and mini-marshmallows.

MENU IDEAS
A perfect treat for any brown bag lunch—no matter if it's for Dad or child.

WHAT CHILDREN CAN DO
Kids can mix batter from start to finish. Use a deep bowl so they don't end up *wearing* too much of it.

Huey, Dewey, and Louie's CHOCOLATE PIE

from Donald's Nephews

uey, Dewey, and Louie made their first appearance on the silver screen in the 1938 short movie Donald's Nephews, *and what an outrageous debut it was! Surely, Donald's house would never be the same again. What better way to calm things down than with a gorgeous pie, sitting right there on the table and waiting to be eaten? But this only leads to further pranks—the kids spike Donald's slice with spicy hot "Volcano Mustard"! Luckily, we've decided to leave the hot stuff out of this recipe. Indeed, this pie contains only ingredients that are as pure and simple as Donald's lovable nephews. Feel that comforting sensation rise as your belly is filled with sweet chocolate, and your heart is soothed. After all, "little children are only angels without wings," correct?*

❝ HERE, UNCA DONALD.

DO YOU WANT SOME PIE? ❞

HOW TO MAKE IT

6 Servings

3 Preparation Time (hours)

INGREDIENTS

PIECRUST

1 lb.	flour
1/4 cup	salt
8 tbs.	unsalted butter
5 tbs.	ice water

FILLING

2 oz.	flour
6 oz.	sugar
2 oz.	unsweetened cocoa powder
1 quart	milk
3	egg yolks
1 tsp.	water
1 tsp.	vanilla extract

NUTRITION INFORMATION

Each Serving Contains

Calories	550
Total fat	26 g
Saturated fat	9 g
Carbohydrates	72 g
Sodium	475 mg
Fiber	3 g
Protein	13 g

PIECRUST

➡ Place flour and salt in the bowl of a food processor, and pulse once or twice to combine. Add butter, and pulse on and off until mixture resembles small peas.

➡ Sprinkle in cold water; then pulse 3-4 times until mixture forms a ball. Remove and divide into two pieces. Shape each one into a disk and refrigerate for about 15 minutes.

➡ When cold, roll out each between 2 sheets of waxed paper into 10-inch circles, and place back in the refrigerator (still wrapped in waxed paper) until ready to use. This may be done a day in advance.

FILLING

➡ Mix flour, 5 ounces of sugar, and cocoa powder in a pot; add milk, and place over medium heat, stirring often. When mixture begins to thicken, stir more often to prevent lumps. Continue for 15 to 20 minutes at a medium simmer. Do not cook on high heat. ▶

NOTES

For a sweeter pie, add more sugar to filling.

MENU IDEAS

A perfect alternative to a birthday cake after someone's favorite meal.

SERVING SUGGESTIONS

A dab of vanilla-flavored whipped cream and a sprinkle of your favorite crumbled candy bar for extra crunch take this pie to a whole new level.

WHAT CHILDREN CAN DO

Little hands can stir the bowl of chocolate pudding over ice; they can also brush the top of the pie shell with the egg mixture and sprinkle it with sugar.

HOW TO MAKE IT

VARIATIONS

This dessert can be made with the same amount of chopped bittersweet chocolate for a more intense chocolate flavor. For a more adult-style pie, spread 2 oz. melted raspberry preserves over filling before covering with upper layer of crust.

➡ Remove 1 ladleful of hot mixture and add to 2 beaten egg yolks. Mix very quickly (this is called tempering).

➡ Add this mixture to the one on the stove. Mix well until it thickens up more, about 3-4 minutes.

➡ Remove to a metal mixing bowl; then place this bowl on top of a bowl of ice, stirring quickly to cool. The result should have the texture of pudding. Keep chilled. Preheat oven to 325°F.

➡ Line a 9-inch pie pan with one piece of dough, trim off excess, then place in preheated oven for 10 to 12 minutes. This is called blind baking the shell, and is done to cook the bottom of the shell a bit before you put in the wet filling and bake it a second time, thus preventing "raw" dough texture and taste at the bottom of the pan.

➡ Remove blind-baked shell, allow to cool slightly, then spoon in chocolate filling and cover with the second piece of dough. Trim ends attractively. Steam vents, as used in fruit pies, are not necessary here.

➡ Combine 1 egg yolk and water, brush on upper crust, then sprinkle with remaining 1 ounce of sugar. Bake in preheated oven for about 25 minutes, or until top turns a light golden brown.

➡ Remove and cool completely before serving, or filling will run.

Winnie the Pooh's

from The Many Adventures of Winnie the Pooh

NO-BAKE HONEY COOKIES

8 Servings

30 Preparation Time (minutes)

INGREDIENTS

8 oz.	vanilla wafer crumbs
1 lb.	confectioners' sugar
10 oz.	pecans, chopped
6 oz.	honey, warmed
6 tbs.	butter, softened
8 oz.	coconut, shredded, toasted

NUTRITION INFORMATION

Each Cookie Contains

Calories	110
Total fat	5 g
Saturated fat	2 g
Sodium	34 mg
Carbohydrates	18 g
Fiber	1 g
Protein	1 g

Combine wafer crumbs, confectioners' sugar, and pecans, mixing well.

➡ In a small bowl, combine softened butter with warm honey; then add to dry mixture, once again mixing thoroughly.

➡ Shape into small balls, about 1 tablespoon each; then roll each in chopped coconut and press lightly to flatten out.

➡ Store in refrigerator.

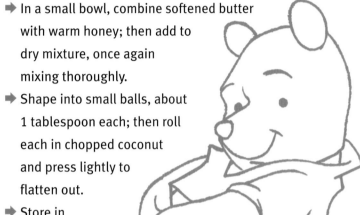

WHAT CHILDREN CAN DO

Kids can participate from start to finish, since cooking and sharp objects are not required.
Have lots of damp towels ready to wipe off messy hands and faces.

66 I'M SO RUMBLY IN MY TUMBLY!
TIME FOR SOMETHING SWEET . . . 99

Tarzan and Jane's

GRILLED TROPICAL FRUITS WITH PASSION FRUIT COULIS

arzan invites Jane to share in the many wonders and beauty of his world, the jungle. He's also well aware that his new companion has a lot to teach him about the "civilized" world. In their honor, this recipe unites his wild and tropical home with her refined and urban culture—he supplies the passion fruit; she supplies the technology! And we're lucky enough to be able to enjoy the best of both worlds in the comfort of our own homes!

> ❝ I WAS SAVED BY A FLYING WILD MAN IN A LOINCLOTH. ❞

HOW TO MAKE IT

4 Servings

30 Preparation Time (minutes)

INGREDIENTS

¹/₂	pineapple, peeled and cored
2	mangoes, pitted
1	ugly fruit, sectioned
1	papaya, halved and seeded
2	bananas, peeled and halved
4 tbs.	sugar
4	passion fruit, pulp only
1	lime
1 tsp.	sugar
4	orchids, for garnish

NUTRITION INFORMATION

Each Serving Contains

Calories	244
Total fat	1 g
Saturated fat	0 g
Carbohydrates	63 g
Sodium	10 mg
Fiber	7 g
Protein	2 g

➡ Preheat broiler. Thickly slice pineapple, and place on broiler pan. Cut mangoes in half, and remove pits. Using the tip of a sharp paring knife, make diamond patterns in flesh, cutting lengthwise and across, leaving skin intact. With both hands, gently "pop" cut up flesh so that skin is now concave, and flesh is exposed in small cubes. Place on broiler pan next to pineapple.

➡ Peel and section ugly fruit into 4 thick slices, and place on broiler pan along with sliced papaya and bananas. Sprinkle all with 4 tablespoons of sugar and place under broiler for a few minutes. You want the fruit lightly colored and bits of sugar slightly caramelized.

➡ Meanwhile, mash passion fruit pulp together with lime juice, add 1 teaspoon of sugar, and mix well.

➡ When fruit looks attractively caramelized and warmed through, remove from broiler and divide among 4 plates. Garnish with small orchids, spooning a bit of sauce on plates as well. Alternatively, garnished fruit may be arranged on a platter with a small bowl containing passion fruit coulis in the middle.

NOTES

If ugly fruit is unavailable, easily substitute pink grapefruit. Orchids are for decoration only—if unavailable, a wedge of lime will suffice.

SERVING SUGGESTIONS

If you can find it, serve with a scoop of either coconut sorbet or coconut ice cream—which will melt slightly when heaped atop the warm grilled fruits.

MENU IDEAS

A fine ending after a small salad and a plate of "Gus the Goose's Spaghetti with Peas."

WHAT CHILDREN CAN DO

Little hands can arrange the completed dish and decorate it with passion fruit sauce and orchids or edible flowers.

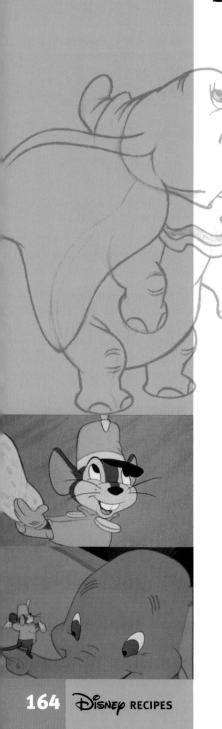

Dumbo's

from Dumbo

ROASTED PEANUT PIE WITH CHOCOLATE

*D*umbo sure is lucky to have a pal like Timothy. Sincere and affectionate, this little guy knows how to boost morale when times are tough. Indeed, if it weren't for him, Dumbo might never have learned to believe in himself enough to fly. If there's someone like Timothy in your life, a special person you can always count on, who believes in you and encourages you to persevere, then why not surprise him or her with a small token of your appreciation? Try this extra special pie that combines two natural "friends"—peanuts and chocolate, which complement each other like Dumbo and Timothy. As sweet as the joys of life, yet as salty as tears, the comfort it provides is worthy of the large, soft, and warm Mrs. Jumbo, brimming with restorative consoling powers.

**❝ LOOK, A PEANUT! COME ON.
EAT IT. GOT LOTS OF VITAMINS.
GIVE YA A LOT OF, UH, PEP. ❞**

HOW TO MAKE IT

8 Servings

2 Preparation Time (hours)

INGREDIENTS

8 oz.	peanuts, raw, shelled
2 oz.	semisweet chocolate
1	10-inch piecrust, prebaked
2 tbs.	unsalted butter room temperature
3	eggs, large, room temperature
1 tsp.	vanilla extract
$^3/_4$ cup	corn syrup, dark
4 oz.	sugar
$^1/_8$ tsp.	salt

NUTRITION INFORMATION

Each Serving Contains

Calories	424
Total fat	22 g
Saturated fat	6 g
Sodium	251 mg
Carbohydrates	54 g
Fiber	0 g
Protein	8 g

➡ Preheat oven to 350°F. Roast peanuts on a baking sheet in preheated oven for 8 to 10 minutes, until lightly browned and fragrant. Remove and let cool.

➡ Melt chocolate until spreadable, then coat the inside of prebaked pie shell, keeping edge of crust clean. Let harden.

➡ Melt butter until liquid (but not separated); then combine with eggs, vanilla, corn syrup, sugar, and salt.

➡ Place peanuts in pie shell. Place on a baking sheet to catch any drips while baking, then slowly pour in liquid.

➡ Bake in preheated oven for 25 to 30 minutes, or until the center shakes slightly while still in oven.

➡ Remove and cool completely before serving.

SERVING SUGGESTIONS

Serve with a dab of fresh whipped cream, while imagining that you are flying high over the world with your best friend.

VARIATIONS

Walnuts, pecans, cashews, almonds, macadamia nuts—or any combination of these—may be used in place of peanuts.

WHAT CHILDREN CAN DO

Little hands can remove peanut shells and skins. Remember to buy twice the amount needed, since quality control calls for sampling nuts.

Maid Marian's

from Robin Hood

BLACKBERRY PIE

Nottingham is the site of a great archery contest, with a kiss from Lady Marian as the most-sought-after prize of all. What a spectacular event it is, complete with brightly colored balloons and stands selling enticing blackberry pies for a mere two pence each. Too bad those pies end up being hurled—albeit by the romantic and determined Maid Marian—in the faces of Robin Hood's adversaries instead of being eaten. Why waste such tasty delicacies? And why spend all that energy fighting when there's so much fun to be had in the kitchen? Maid Marian's blackberry pie is a snap to make. For something a bit more risqué, cut out "lips" from the second piece of pastry, bake separately, then cover the baked pie with these kisses for your own special Robin Hood or Maid Marian.

❝ WELL, USUALLY, THE HERO GIVES HIS FAIR LADY A KISS. ❞

HOW TO MAKE IT

8 Servings

3 Preparation Time
(hours)

INGREDIENTS

PIECRUST

16 oz.	flour
8 tbs.	unsalted butter, room temperature
3 oz.	shortening, room temperature
1 tsp.	salt
1 tsp.	sugar
1 tsp.	cold water
1	egg yolk
2 tsps.	vinegar
$^1/_4$ cup	cold water

FILLING

2 lb.	blackberries, fresh or frozen
7 oz.	sugar
2 oz.	flour
$^1/_4$ tsp.	salt
$^1/_4$ tsp.	freshly grated ginger
1 tb.	heavy cream

PIECRUST

➡ In a food processor, combine flour, butter, shortening, salt, sugar, and 1 teaspoon of water until crumbly. In a small separate bowl, combine well egg yolk, vinegar, and $^1/_4$ cup cold water.

➡ Pour egg mixture into food processor bowl and pulse 5-6 seconds until just combined. Remove from bowl and divide in two. Wrap each in plastic wrap and refrigerate for at least 1 hour, or up to 1 day.

➡ Roll out one piece to fit pie pan, line pan, then refrigerate until filling is ready. Preheat oven to 350°F. Roll out second piece of dough, same size as first piece, and refrigerate.

FILLING

➡ In a large bowl, combine blackberries, 6 ounces of sugar, flour, salt, and ginger, mixing well. Pour into pastry-lined shell.

➡ Remove flat dough from refrigerator, place over berry-filled pie shell, and crimp edges attractively.

➡ Place pie on a baking sheet to catch any spills during baking.

➡ Combine cream and remaining sugar, then brush on top of pie; bake 30-35 minutes. When done, upper crust should be golden brown. Remove from oven, and allow to cool $1^1/_2$ hours before serving.

NUTRITION INFORMATION

Each Serving Contains

Calories	450
Total fat	22 g
Saturated fat	12 g
Sodium	452 mg
Carbohydrates	60 g
Fiber	4 g
Protein	5 g

NOTES

If using frozen berries, allow an extra 10 minutes, baking time.

VARIATIONS

Instead of blackberries, try cranberries, raspberries, blueberries, or any combination of berries, and continue as above.

MENU IDEAS

Take this pie on a picnic in the woods, along with some hearty sandwiches and a bowl of "Stromboli's Penne with Grilled Vegetables."

WHAT CHILDREN CAN DO

Children can mix the filling and crimp the edges of the piecrust together.

Fauna's
BIRTHDAY CAKE

from Sleeping Beauty

In the sixteen years that the three good fairies have been entrusted with the care of Briar Rose, they haven't learned much about how mortals get along with life's day-to-day activities. It isn't until the princess's sixteenth birthday that they realize they've got some catching up to do. Desperate and tired, they rely on the help of their magic wands to save the day (and the cake) before Briar Rose returns. In the end, though, "aunt" Fauna's creation looks astonishingly tasty. Bake it for the birthday of someone you love—your friend will have a hard time forgetting such an affectionate gesture. A bit of practice can work wonders, even without the aid of a magic wand. But remember: don't imitate Fauna while preparing the batter!

❝ NOW, YEAST, ONE TSP. "TSP."? OH, ONE TEASPOON, OF COURSE! ❞

HOW TO MAKE IT

10 Servings
3½ Preparation Time (hours)

INGREDIENTS

16 tbs.	butter
1 lb.	flour
1 lb.	sugar
²/₃ tsp.	salt
2 tsp.	baking powder
1 cup	milk
2 tsp.	vanilla extract
5	egg whites

FROSTING/FILLING

8 oz.	white chocolate, finely chopped
4 tbs.	unsalted butter
24 oz.	sour cream, room temperature
4 tbs.	raspberry eau-de-vie
1 tsp.	grated orange rind red food coloring blue food coloring

➡ Preheat oven to 325°F. Coat 2 round layer cake pans with a bit of butter and flour, then line with parchment paper.

➡ Combine all dry ingredients. Add 16 tbs. butter; combine with mixer until mix resembles bread crumbs. In another bowl, combine milk, vanilla, and egg whites. Then slowly add wet mix to dry. Combine well.

➡ Scrape down sides of bowl; then mix on high for about 30 seconds. Scrape down sides of bowl again; mix on high for about 10 more seconds. Divide batter evenly between the two baking pans.

➡ Bake in preheated oven for 25 minutes, or until an inserted toothpick comes out clean. Remove from oven and allow to cool for about 20 minutes. Remove layers from pans and cool completely before frosting.

NUTRITION INFORMATION

Each Serving Contains

Calories	847
Total fat	46 g
Saturated fat	28 g
Sodium	559 mg
Carbohydrates	100 g
Fiber	1 g
Protein	11 g

MENU IDEAS
This layer cake may be served in the afternoon with tea to celebrate someone's birthday.

SERVING SUGGESTIONS
Instead of ice cream, garnish with sliced and slightly sugared fruit, such as peaches, nectarines, strawberries, or bananas.

WHAT CHILDREN CAN DO
Kids can and should provide their own personal touch when it comes to the most important part of the recipe – decorating the cake!

HOW TO MAKE IT

NOTES
This recipe is for 2-layer cake.
For a 4-layer cake like the one
in the illustration below,
increase doses for batter and
frosting/filling by $1/2$ for the
2 smaller pans.

FROSTING/FILLING

➡ Double-boil chopped white chocolate in a metal bowl over a pot of simmering hot water, stirring constantly with a rubber spatula to melt evenly. Simmering water must not touch the bottom of the bowl. Add butter.

➡ Alternatively, melt white chocolate and 2 ounces of butter in a microwave, stirring every 10 seconds until very soft but not liquid.

➡ Mix well with a whip, then add sour cream at room temperature. Mix well. Add raspberry eau-de-vie. Remove $1/3$ of the frosting and add grated orange rind (keep it white for the filling).

➡ Remove $1/4$ of the remaining frosting to a smaller bowl and tint pink; tint the remainder of the frosting a pleasant shade of blue. Place one layer upside down on serving platter or cardboard disk.

➡ Spread white frosting on top of this layer. Trim second layer so that it sits flat. Place second layer with cut side flush against frosted bottom layer.

➡ Cover sides and top of cake with blue frosting. Decorate with pink frosting, as shown below. Refrigerate for several hours; remove from refrigerator about 1 hour prior to serving.

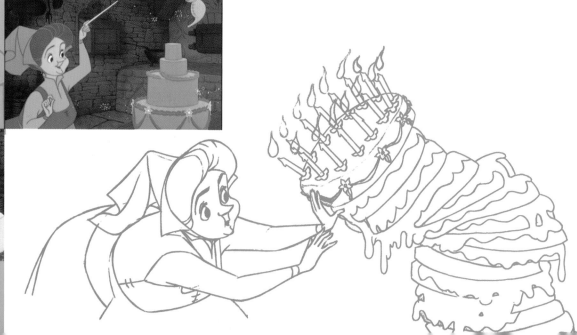

King Louie's

BANANAS WITH HONEY AND COCONUT

4 Servings

20 Preparation Time (minutes)

INGREDIENTS

6 oz.	honey
4	bananas
2 oz.	shredded coconut

eat a nonstick pan until very hot, add honey, and bring to a boil. Peel bananas and slice lengthwise; add to boiling honey. Cook on high 1-2 minutes; then turn and remove from heat.

➡ Divide bananas among 4 small plates; spoon over hot honey.

➡ Garnish each with a sprinkling of coconut.

NUTRITION INFORMATION

Each Serving Contains

Calories	258
Total fat	7 g
Saturated fat	4 g
Sodium	9 mg
Carbohydrates	53 g
Fiber	2 g
Protein	1 g

NOTES
Add roasted and chopped nuts as well.

SERVING SUGGESTIONS
Top with whipped cream just before serving.

MENU IDEAS
This simple dessert is wonderful after grilled halibut steaks and a side of "Fun and Fancy Free's Ratatouille."

WHAT CHILDREN CAN DO

Kids love peeling and slicing bananas. Also, with a safety potato peeler, older children can shred fresh coconuts if available—after parents remove the shells and meat, of course.

❝ HAVE A BANANA!

HAVE TWO BANANAS! ❞

Goofy's BIRTHDAY CAKE

from Mickey's Birthday Party

In the short movie Mickey's Birthday Party *(1942), Mickey's many friends arrange a truly magnificent celebration, and it's up to Goofy to prepare a cake worthy of the occasion. Predictably, he makes a thorough mess of the job—and the kitchen!—so what else can he do but run to the nearest bakery and buy a ready-made cake? Follow our instructions and we guarantee you a cake that will bring down the house with applause. It is light, moist, and delicately flavored, with a slightly tangy, sweet frosting that is never heavy and cloying—as fresh and bright as the enduring friendship between Mickey and Goofy.*

66 HAPPY BIRTHDAY, MICKEY! 99

HOW TO MAKE IT

8	Servings
3	Preparation Time (hours)

INGREDIENTS

1 tb.	butter
23 oz.	cake flour
5	egg yolks
18 oz.	sugar
$\frac{1}{3}$ cup	water
1 tsp.	vanilla extract
16	egg whites
$\frac{2}{3}$ tb.	cream of tartar

FROSTING

12 oz.	white chocolate, chopped
16 oz.	cream cheese, softened
16 tbs.	unsalted butter, room temperature
1 tb.	raspberry eau-de-vie
	food coloring, your choice of color

NUTRITION INFORMATION

Each Serving Contains

Calories	1,126
Total fat	61 g
Saturated fat	36 g
Sodium	294 mg
Carbohydrates	133 g
Fiber	3 g
Protein	19 g

➡ Preheat oven to 350°F. Coat three 8-inch round cake pans with a bit of butter and flour; then line with parchment paper.

➡ Beat egg yolks and $\frac{1}{4}$ of the sugar, at medium speed, until they form a ribbon when beaters are removed from bowl, about 12 minutes.

➡ Combine flour and remaining sugar in a small bowl. Continuing to mix egg yolks at low speed, slowly add water and vanilla. Increase speed to medium.

➡ Slowly add flour mixture while continuing to mix at medium speed.

➡ In a separate bowl with clean beaters, beat egg whites until a soft peak is formed, add cream of tartar and beat for an additional 30 seconds or so. Fold egg whites into batter, then pour batter into prepared pans.

➡ Place immediately in preheated oven. Bake 22 minutes before opening oven. Check for doneness with a toothpick, which should come out clean when inserted in cake.

➡ Remove from oven and allow to cool for about 20 minutes. Remove cakes from pans and cool completely before frosting.

SERVING SUGGESTIONS
Best served with scoops of strawberry ice cream.

MENU IDEAS
The perfect dessert after an entrée as American as Goofy himself, "Ichabod's Roast Turkey with Giblet Gravy."

WHAT CHILDREN CAN DO

Kids can help frost and decorate the birthday cake.

HOW TO MAKE IT

FROSTING

➡ Prepare frosting while cake is cooling. Double-boil chopped white chocolate in a metal bowl over a pot of simmering hot water, stirring constantly with a rubber spatula to melt evenly. Simmering water must not touch the bottom of the bowl. Alternatively, melt white chocolate in a microwave, stirring every 20 seconds or so. In any case, avoid splashing water in the chocolate, or it will curdle irreparably.

➡ In another bowl, beat cream cheese with a handheld mixer until smooth and light. Slowly mix in melted white chocolate, followed by softened butter. Once all has been incorporated, mix in raspberry eau-de-vie.

➡ Remove about $1/2$ cup of frosting to keep white for decorating, and tint the rest with food coloring of your choice.

➡ Frost cake and decorate as shown on the previous page—but, please, be more careful than Goofy was!

Elliott's
CARAMELIZED RED APPLES

from Pete's Dragon

Preheat oven to 350°F. Core apples completely and remove peel from top third of each. Run the tip of the knife crosswise along the middle of apples to help prevent them from splitting during baking. Place in a pan that will hold 4 apples snugly.

➡ Combine sugar with cinnamon and nutmeg; fill apple cavities with mixture. Place $1/2$ teaspoon of butter on the top of each one.

➡ Bake for 22 to 25 minutes, or until lightly golden and easily pierced with the tip of small knife. Do not overcook, or you will have applesauce.

4 Servings

45 Preparation Time (minutes)

INGREDIENTS

4	apples
4 oz.	brown sugar
$1/4$ tsp.	ground cinnamon
$1/8$ tsp.	ground nutmeg
2 tsps.	unsalted butter

NUTRITION INFORMATION

Each Serving Contains

Calories	497
Total fat	27 g
Saturated fat	16 g
Sodium	404 mg
Carbohydrates	60 g
Fiber	3 g
Protein	5 g

❝ MMM, YOU'RE A GOOD COOK, ELLIOTT! I KNOW HOW YOU FEEL, BUT YOU'LL HAVE TO MAKE YOURSELF INVISIBLE. ❞

NOTES

Best made with a tart, firm red cooking apple. Rome and Cortland varieties are perfect, though Golden Delicious and Granny Smiths work equally well.

SERVING SUGGESTIONS

Serve on a small plate, garnished with a small spoonful of either sour cream or crème fraîche and one small cookie for textural variation. Use smaller apples or halve larger ones and use as a garnish for pork roast.

WHAT CHILDREN CAN DO

Older kids can peel the apples, using a safety peeler.

Johnny Appleseed's

APPLE PIE

American folk hero Johnny Appleseed planted apple trees wherever he roamed. In one scene from the Disney film version of this legend, he is visited by an angel who reminds him: "Think of all the good things that can be made from apples and right now there are no apple trees out there in the wilderness."

So he nurtures tiny seedlings into young trees and distributes them among settlers as they head westward. In another scene, pioneers celebrate the apple harvest with foods from those very same trees. What better way, then, to honor Johnny Appleseed than with a classic apple pie?

> **"Aaaand what's wrong with apples, if you please? Ain't they 'bout the finest fruit in all the land?"**

HOW TO MAKE IT

8 Servings

2 Preparation Time (hours)

INGREDIENTS

PIECRUST

20 oz.	flour
2 tsps.	granulated sugar
1/2 tsp.	salt
16 tbs.	unsalted butter, cubed
6 tbs.	water, ice cold

FILLING

6	apples, peeled and cored
1 tb.	lemon juice
7 oz.	brown sugar
1/4 tsp.	nutmeg
1/2 tsp.	cinnamon
1/8 tsp.	ground allspice
1 tbs.	flour
1	egg yolk

NUTRITION INFORMATION

Each Serving Contains

Calories	495
Total fat	27 g
Saturated fat	16 g
Sodium	404 mg
Carbohydrates	60 g
Fiber	3 g
Protein	5 g

PIECRUST

➡ Preheat oven to 400°F. Sift flour, sugar, and salt into the bowl of a food processor. Add butter and process 4-5 seconds until mixture is just combined, resembling small pebbles and sand.

➡ Add 3 tablespoons of ice water and process 2 seconds. Once again, add 2 tablespoons water and process 2 seconds. Mixture should become one ball of dough. If necessary, add final tablespoon of water and process for 2 more seconds. Remove dough and cut into 2 equal portions. Wrap one portion in plastic wrap; set aside.

➡ On a lightly floured work surface, roll the other portion of dough out to form a 10-inch circle, 1/4 inch thick. Roll back onto rolling pin and fit dough into pie pan. Blind bake pie shell in preheated oven for 10 to 12 minutes.

➡ Roll second piece of dough out, also 1/4 inch thick and 10 inches in diameter. Place rolled-out dough in refrigerator.

FILLING

➡ Slice peeled apples thinly from top to bottom and place in large mixing bowl. Add lemon juice, 6 ounces of brown sugar, nutmeg, cinnamon, allspice, and flour. Remove pie shell from oven, allow to cool briefly. Add apple mixture, smoothing out evenly.

➡ Place second piece of dough on top; crimp edges attractively.

➡ Combine well egg yolk and 1 ounce of brown sugar. Brush over top of pie; then cut several steam vents in center.

➡ Place pie on a baking sheet to catch drips; then move into preheated oven. Bake for 12 minutes at 400°F. Then turn oven down to 350°F, continuing to bake for 20 to 25 minutes.

NOTES

Apples that work best for this pie are the firm and hard varieties, like Granny Smith, Rome, Golden Delicious, or Spy, just to name a few. Pie dough may be prepared a few days in advance and kept refrigerated.

SERVING SUGGESTIONS

For a special treat, place a thin slice of cheddar cheese on top of a warm slice of pie, as was the custom in the 1800s.

VARIATIONS

You might try mixing the spices into the crust, and mix apples with just sugar and lemon juice for a very simple variation.

MENU IDEAS

This, along with pumpkin pie, is a classic Thanksgiving dessert.

The Mad Hatter and March Hare's
from Alice in Wonderland
CHEESECAKE

*D*on't forget to invite your more eccentric friends to your next tea party, but keep the "muthtard"—as Mad Hatter would so emphatically say—and mallets out of sight in order to protect your watches. And don't spare the cheesecake—a dessert elegant enough for the Queen of Hearts, as colorful as the Mad Hatter's hat, and as zany as the March Hare himself. It's bound to be your ace in the hole, so to speak. Should any of your guests become overly rowdy, you know the remedy: a dab of jam on the nose will calm things down, as the Dormouse, who is fond of hiding in sugar bowls, can attest. One last word of advice for guests: remember to be invited, since "it's very rude (indeed!) to sit at the table if you're not."

" MUSTAAAAAAAAARD!" "MUSTARD, YES!" "DON'T LET'S BE SILLY! LEMON — THAT'S DIFFERENT!" "THAT'S — THERE! "

HOW TO MAKE IT

10 Servings

3 Preparation Time (hours)

INGREDIENTS

10 oz.	graham cracker crumbs
4 oz.	almonds, roasted and ground
4 oz.	brown sugar
2 tbs.	butter, softened
1 lb.	ricotta cheese
1 lb.	cream cheese, softened
12 oz.	granulated sugar
4	eggs
2 tbs.	vanilla extract
3 tbs.	all-purpose flour
3 tbs.	cornstarch
4 tbs.	butter, melted
1 pint	crème fraîche
6	kiwis, peeled
1 pint	strawberries, hulled

NUTRITION INFORMATION

Each Serving Contains

Calories	676
Total fat	43 g
Saturated fat	25 g
Sodium	369 mg
Carbohydrates	62 g
Fiber	3 g
Protein	15 g

➡ Combine graham cracker crumbs, almonds, brown sugar, and 2 tbs. softened butter well. Grease the side of a springform pan, press mixture into the bottom, and refrigerate until needed.

➡ Preheat oven to 325°F. Blend ricotta and cream cheese; gradually add granulated sugar, combining well. Add eggs one at a time, beating well after adding each. Stir in vanilla.

➡ Sift flour and cornstarch, then sift again over cheese mixture, and blend well. Add melted butter and mix until smooth. Blend in crème fraîche. Pour into greased springform pan. Bake for 1 hour. Turn off oven and let cake remain 2 more hours without opening oven door.

➡ Remove from oven and chill. When cold, slide a very thin knife around the edge of pan to loosen cake from side before removing.

➡ When ready to serve, process peeled kiwis in a food processor or blender until smooth; sweeten with a bit of sugar if desired. Rinse out machine and do the same with the strawberries. Cover top of cheesecake with kiwi puree; after slicing, spoon strawberry sauce alongside.

MENU IDEAS
A royal finish to a special meal of King Hubert's Veal Roast with Apricots and Thyme and steamed asparagus.

NOTES
If graham cracker crumbs are not available, substitute with a simple dry cookie/biscuit.

VARIATIONS
Use pecans in place of almonds and add 2 teaspoons of butter extract and 2 teaspoons of rum extract.

SERVING SUGGESTIONS
Great at a tea party in small portions. Offer a piece of cake to anyone who compliments your singing. Always have plenty of clean teacups and empty chairs.

Tigger's

from The Tigger Movie

"T FROZEN DARK CHOCOLATE ORANGE MOUSSE

he most wonderful thing about Tigger is that "I'm the only one." The same goes for this dish—it's one of a kind. Like Tigger himself, it's smart and somewhat boisterous, but this dessert won't "bounce" you about as this crazy character might do. It provides that nice, warm, fuzzy feeling, especially when you share it with your friends, just as Tigger, Pooh, Christopher Robin, Owl, Piglet, Roo, and Kanga might have enjoyed it together. Why, this treat would even cheer up ol' Eeyore, and is synonymous with sharing the wealth and spreading love.

" RULE THREE. NEVER BOUNCE RIGHT AFTER EATIN', OR YOU'LL GET TAIL CRAMPS. "

HOW TO MAKE IT

4 Servings

1½ Preparation Time (minutes)

INGREDIENTS

6 oz.	bittersweet chocolate, chopped fine
6	eggs, separated
8 oz.	heavy cream, cold
2 tbs.	sugar
1 tb.	vanilla extract
¼ tsp.	salt
1 tsp.	finely grated orange rind
1 tbs.	orange liqueur

OPTIONAL GARNISH

6	orange rind strips
4 oz.	heavy cream

NUTRITION INFORMATION

Each Serving Contains

Calories	544
Total fat	41 g
Saturated fat	23 g
Sodium	241 mg
Carbohydrates	40 g
Fiber	3 g
Protein	11 g

➡ Melt chocolate in a heavy pan or in a microwave, stirring every 20 seconds or so until smooth. If melting over hot water, bottom of bowl must not touch the water.

➡ Remove from heat and add egg yolks one at a time, beating well after each addition, with handheld mixer on high speed. In a separate bowl, beat egg whites until stiff; then refrigerate.

➡ In another bowl, beat cream, sugar, vanilla, salt, and orange rind until stiff; then add liqueur.

➡ Fold whipped cream and egg whites together gently. Hold ¼ aside; fold chocolate into remaining egg/cream mixture. Layer chocolate and orange mousse into parfait glasses like tiger stripes; then place in freezer.

➡ May be prepared several days in advance. Once frozen, wrap each glass with plastic wrap to prevent mousse from absorbing freezer odors. Remove from freezer 10 minutes before serving.

➡ Whip cream until soft peaks form; then place a dollop on top of each mousse and garnish with a knot made from orange rind strips.

VARIATIONS

Make with cherry liqueur, replacing orange rind garnish with a brandied cherry.

MENU IDEAS

This dessert would be a wonderful ending to an extra special meal. Start things out with "Philoctetes' Onion Marmalade with Raisins." Follow with lamb chops and "Pocahontas's Savory Indian Corn Pudding"—then a short break before serving dessert.

WHAT CHILDREN CAN DO

Let kids whip the cream and be in charge of garnish knot-tying.

Witch Hazel's
PUMPKIN PIE

*I*n the short movie Trick or Treat *(1952), lovable, wacky Witch Hazel joins up with Huey, Dewey, and Louie to play a few tricks on their crotchety uncle Donald. She uses her knowledge of magic to conjure up a potion able to bring pumpkin masks terrifyingly to life and turn solid fence posts into ghosts. If you ask us, she should have used her spells in the kitchen to prepare special treats for Halloween. Try working a little of your own magic with this zippy version of a classic autumnal dessert: all you need is an open mind and willingness to try something new. Be daring and see whether your guests reward you with a trick or a treat!*

❝ **TRICK OR TREAT FOR HALLOWEEN, BETTER GIVE A TREAT THAT'S GOOD TO EAT, IF YOU GONNA KEEP LIFE SERENE! KIDS! THE STUFF'S LOOOOADED!** ❞

HOW TO MAKE IT

8 Servings

2 Preparation Time (hours)

INGREDIENTS

PIECRUST

8 oz.	flour
$1/4$ tsp.	salt
1 tsp.	New Mexico chili powder
4 tbs.	butter
3 tbs.	ice water

FILLING

4 oz.	cream cheese, room temperature
3 tbs.	finely chopped candied gingerroot
15 oz.	canned pumpkin puree
14 oz.	canned condensed sweetened milk
2	eggs, separated
$1/4$ tsp.	ground cinnamon
$1/4$ tsp.	ground nutmeg
$1/4$ tsp.	ground cloves
$1/4$ tsp.	salt

TOPPING

2 tbs.	flour
2 oz.	brown sugar
$1/2$ tsp.	finely ground black pepper
2 tbs.	butter
4 oz.	hazelnuts, coarsely chopped

PIECRUST

➡ Place flour, salt, and chili powder in the bowl of a food processor. Pulse once or twice to combine. Add butter, pulsing on and off until mixture resembles small peas.

➡ Sprinkle in cold water and pulse 3-4 times until mixture forms a ball. Remove and refrigerate for about 15 minutes.

➡ When chilled, roll out to $1/4$-inch thickness, about 10 inches in diameter. Roll onto rolling pin, then fit into pie pan, and uniformly finish edges. Refrigerate until needed. This may be done a day or two in advance.

FILLING

➡ Preheat oven to 425°F. Prick bottom of shell with a fork to prevent it from rising during baking.

➡ Blind bake shell for 10 to 12, minutes or until lightly browned; then allow to cool. In a small bowl, combine cream cheese with candied ginger, then spread on prebaked piecrust, being careful not to break crust.

➡ In a large bowl, mix pumpkin, sweetened condensed milk, and egg yolks. Stir in cinnamon, nutmeg, cloves, and salt.

➡ In a separate large bowl, whip egg whites until soft peaks are formed. Fold into pumpkin mixture and pour filling into piecrust. Bake for 15 minutes in preheated oven.

TOPPING

➡ While pie is baking, prepare topping. In a small bowl, combine flour, brown sugar, and black pepper. Blend in cold butter with a fork until mixture is crumbly. Mix in chopped hazelnuts. Sprinkle topping over pie after baking for 15 minutes. Reduce heat to 350°F; bake for an additional 40 minutes, or until set.

NUTRITION INFORMATION

Each Serving Contains

Calories	1,480
Total fat	22 g
Saturated fat	12 g
Sodium	379 mg
Carbohydrates	315 g
Fiber	2 g
Protein	12 g

VARIATIONS

Other nuts may be used in the topping, or, if you prefer, removed completely. Substitute black pepper in the crust with ground cardamom for a sweeter, milder topping.

MENU IDEAS

Try a bowl of "Cookie's Special Chili" and some cold "Heroes' Herculade" to drink before a slice of this pie.

WHAT CHILDREN CAN DO

Little hands can combine cream cheese with candied ginger, and mix ingredients for the topping.

Santa's COOKIES

Reading all those "Dear Santa" letters and personally making sure all the toys made by his elves are up to standard, Santa must work up quite an appetite. And by the size of his belly, we'd say he indulges himself fairly regularly. This holiday season, tempt Santa with an all-new cookie, whose cheery goodness is certain to be a big hit not only with Saint Nick but with all his many fans around the world. This minty-crunchy-chocolaty combo is easy to prepare and can be made in advance. We'll bet even Santa has never tasted the likes of these yummy cookies before. Remember to place them next to a cold glass of milk for his proper enjoyment.

" AHAHAHAHAHAHAHÀÀÀÀ! MERRY CHRISTMAS TO ALL, AND TO ALL A GOOD NIGHT! "

HOW TO MAKE IT

4	Servings
2	Preparation Time (hours)

INGREDIENTS

16 tbs.	butter, room temperature
8 oz.	confectioners' sugar
1	egg
1 tsp.	vanilla extract
1 tsp.	almond extract
1 tsp.	salt
20 oz.	flour
8 oz.	peppermint candies, crushed
4 oz.	dark chocolate

NUTRITION INFORMATION

Each Serving Contains

Calories	159
Total fat	9 g
Saturated fat	5 g
Sodium	169 mg
Carbohydrates	18 g
Fiber	1 g
Protein	2 g

➡ Preheat oven to 350°F. Combine butter and confectioners' sugar into a creamy mixture. Incorporate egg and flavor extracts; then add salt and 20 ounces of flour, plus half the crushed candies. Mix until dough is smooth.

➡ Add more flour if dough is a bit sticky. Then split the mixture into 2 logs, roll each in plastic, and refrigerate until firm, about 30 minutes.

➡ Slice into rounds about $1/3$ inch thick, and place on parchment-lined cookie sheets. Bake in preheated oven for 8 to 10 minutes. Cookies are done when firm but not browned.

➡ Remove from the paper-lined trays and cool completely. Repeat until all cookies are done.

➡ When all cookies have cooled, melt chocolate in a microwave until smooth, dip half of each cookie into melted chocolate, then place back on parchment paper and sprinkle chocolate portion with crushed peppermint candy. When completely cool, store in airtight tins away from heat.

BEVERAGE SUGGESTIONS

Accompany with ice-cold milk, served in the fanciest glass you have.

VARIATIONS

Remove vanilla and almond extracts from dough and add 2 tablespoons of cocoa powder; for dipping, use white chocolate.

MENU IDEAS

Serve these cookies with frothy hot cocoa and marshmallows floating on top.

WHAT CHILDREN CAN DO

This is a great recipe for all children to help with. Young ones can crush the peppermint candy in large zip-lock plastic bags, help dip cookies in the melted chocolate, and sprinkle candy pieces on top of cookies. Older children can help mix the dough.

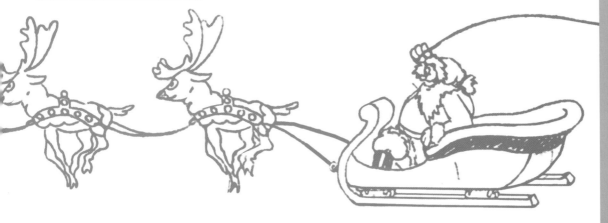

Chip and Dale's

CORN "CHIPS"

In almost all of their shorts, Chip and Dale work out stratagems to augment their hollow-tree pantry with nut-filled goodies—walnuts, hazelnuts, and peanuts are their favorites— and even tasty "extras" like pancakes or popcorn. All this usually takes place amid amusing and pernicious battles waged to the detriment of Pluto or Donald Duck. I especially like to remember the 1951 cartoon Corn Chips, loaded with gags involving the use of popcorn. . .soooooooo, I have decided to create a delicious "chip" in honor of these two endearing chipmunks, with popcorn and peanuts.

" HEY, DALE, WHAT DO YOU SAY?
THINK WE SHOULD EAT THESE NUTS? "

HOW TO MAKE IT

4 Servings

30 Preparation Time (minutes)

INGREDIENTS

2 tbs.	butter
8 oz.	sugar
5 oz.	corn syrup, light
$\frac{1}{2}$ tsp.	baking soda
1 tsp.	water
2 oz.	peanuts
2 quarts	popcorn

NUTRITION INFORMATION

Each Serving Contains

Calories	574
Total fat	21 g
Saturated fat	6 g
Carbohydrates	97 g
Sodium	464 mg
Fiber	4 g
Protein	7 g

➡ Melt butter over low heat in a large saucepan; then add 8 ounces of sugar and 5 ounces of corn syrup. Bring to a boil for about a minute, stirring constantly.

➡ Dissolve baking soda in water.

➡ Remove syrup from heat and add baking soda to mixture— it will foam up.

➡ When it stops foaming, add peanuts and quickly pour over popcorn, mixing fast and well.

➡ Pour batter onto a greased pan, flattening to $\frac{1}{2}$-inch thickness with the buttered back of a square cake pan. Let stand at room temperature, allowing to cool to the touch before cutting triangle-shaped chips.

NOTES
You can also grease your hands with butter or oil and shape batter into balls. Roll them quickly before they set or break into small clusters, and allow to cool on an oiled baking sheet.

VARIATIONS
Different nuts, such as almonds, and hazelnuts or even sunflower seeds may be used in place of walnuts.

MENU IDEAS
Best served with cold soda and pretzels while watching old movies.

WHAT CHILDREN CAN DO

Older kids can shape batter and cut chips. Make sure they're wearing thick rubber gloves to protect their hands from being burned.

Snow White's

from Snow White and the Seven Dwarfs

GOOSEBERRY PIE

now White knows just the thing to show her gratitude to the Seven Dwarfs, who so generously welcomed her into their humble home: a delicious gooseberry pie. In one of the film's most unforgettable scenes, even her animal friends lend a helping hand in creating this dish. Love and compassion are the two basic ingredients for all successful recipes, and it's clear that Snow White offers both in abundance as she turns out this dessert— which, by the way, is probably the most famous pie in the history of cinema. I bet you can't wait to sink your teeth in it!

" C–CAN YOU MAKE DAPPLE LUMPKINS?"
"UH, LUMPLE DAPPLINS?" "APPLE DUMPLINGS!"
"EH, YES!" "CRAPPLE DUMPKINS."
"YES, AND PLUM PUDDING AND GOOSEBERRY PIE."
"GOOSEBERRY PIE? HOORAY! SHE STAYS! "

HOW TO MAKE IT

8 Servings

2¹/₂ Preparation Time (hours)

INGREDIENTS

PASTRY DOUGH

20 oz.	flour, sifted
2 tsp.	sugar
¹/₂ tsp.	salt
18 tbs.	unsalted butter, cubed
6 tbs.	water, ice cold

FILLING

24 oz.	gooseberries, stemmed and washed
17 oz.	sugar
¹/₂ tsp.	grated gingerroot
¹/₄ tsp.	salt
3 tbs.	tapioca, quick-cooking
1 tb.	unsalted butter
2 tbs.	milk

NUTRITION INFORMATION

Each Serving Contains

Calories	626
Total fat	28 g
Saturated fat	17 g
Sodium	482 mg
Carbohydrates	92 g
Fiber	3 g
Protein	5 g

PASTRY DOUGH

➡ Sift flour, sugar, and salt into the bowl of a food processor. Add butter and process until the mixture is just combined, about 4-5 seconds. It should look like small pebbles or sand.

➡ Add 3 tablespoons of ice water and process about 2 seconds; then add 2 tablespoons more water and process 2 more seconds. The mixture should become one ball of dough; if not, add a final tablespoon of water, processing for an additional 2 seconds.

➡ Remove dough and cut into 2 equal portions; cover each with plastic wrap. Refrigerate for about 1 hour.

➡ Roll one piece of dough out ¹/₄ inch thick, about 10 inches in diameter, on a lightly floured board. Fit rolled dough onto the bottom of pie pan, trimming off excess around the edges. Roll out the second piece of dough, also ¹/₄ inch thick and 10 inch in diameter. Place both the rolled and fitted pie dough in the refrigerator for at least 1 hour. Dough may also be refrigerated overnight.

NOTES
Best served within a day or two.

SERVING SUGGESTIONS
Serve with vanilla ice cream or sweetened crème fraîche.

VARIATIONS
A mixture of blueberries, strawberries, and raspberries makes a great variation.

WHAT CHILDREN CAN DO
If you don't have the help of little birds and squirrels in your kitchen, get the kids to crimp the edges of the crust with a fork and cut steam vents in the top of the dough. They can also roll out scraps of dough to write "Grumpy" on the top of the pie.

HOW TO MAKE IT

FILLING

➡ Preheat oven to 350°F. Roughly crush 2 ounces of gooseberries and combine with 16 ounces of sugar, ginger, salt, and tapioca in a 2-quart saucepan. Bring to a boil, cooking until sugar is dissolved. Add remaining gooseberries and continue to cook until they burst.

➡ Remove from heat and add butter. Pour into dough-lined pie pan and top with remaining crust. Trim off excess. If you don't have little birds to help you, crimp edges decoratively with the tines of a fork to resemble their footprints; then cut several steam vents in the pastry top.

➡ Reroll scraps of dough and cut into little strips. Decorate top with the word "Grumpy," just as Snow White did with the help of her squirrel friends.

➡ Brush top with milk, sprinkle with the remaining 1 ounce sugar. Place on a foil-lined cookie sheet to catch drips. Bake in preheated oven for about 35 minutes or until top turns a light golden brown. Remove and allow to cool for 3 hours before serving.

Baked goods

Aladdin's

RICE PUDDING

A mixture of opposites—rice and salt, pistachio nuts and orange blossom water—can be nurtured with love and tenderness to create an alluring dish that recalls the spice-scented air of the open market in Agrabah, pearl of the Orient, city of mystery and enchantment. Only someone with "a heart as pure as an uncut diamond," like Aladdin, could have inspired this concoction. But you don't need to rub a magic lamp to get the Genie to give you the recipe—just look below and take off on your own magic carpet ride. Just as Aladdin promises to share his exciting new world with Jasmine, I too welcome you to an all new world of culinary surprises.

> **66 AND NOW, ESTEEMED EFFENDI, WE FEAST! ALL RIGHT! 99**

HOW TO MAKE IT

4 Servings

1 Preparation Time (hour)

INGREDIENTS

4 oz.	Jasmine rice*
1 quart	milk
1/8 tsp.	salt
4	whole cardamom pods
10 oz.	sugar
3 drops	orange blossom water
3 drops	rose water
2 oz.	dried apricot halves, diced
1 oz.	pistachio nuts

*Jasmine rice is available at Asian markets.

NUTRITION INFORMATION

Each Serving Contains

Calories	568
Total fat	11 g
Saturated fat	6 g
Carbohydrates	110 g
Sodium	191 mg
Fiber	2 g
Protein	12 g

➡ Combine rice, milk, salt, cardamom, and sugar in a 2-quart saucepan.

➡ Simmer partially covered over medium heat for about 1 hour. Stir often, until rice is soft and most of the milk has been absorbed. Do not boil.

➡ Alternatively, you may put the mixture into a partly covered ovenproof dish, and bake in a preheated 350°F oven, also for about an hour, until rice is soft. If it remains slightly hard, add milk and continue to cook until soft.

➡ Remove from stove or oven. Add orange blossom water, rose water, and dried apricots. Mix well. This dish may be served hot or cold. Garnish with pistachios before serving.

NOTES

If you can't locate Jasmine rice, you may also use Basmati Arborio or plain white rice. Orange blossom water is available at Middle Eastern import stores.

MENU IDEAS

A grand finale to a meal that begins with "Mushu's Egg Rolls and Juk," followed by "Mulan's Mahogany Chicken."

SERVING SUGGESTIONS

To give an extra special start to a family member's birthday, serve hot rice pudding for breakfast, and garnish with his or her favorite fresh fruit. Pack some in your children's lunch boxes or sneak it in a plastic bag into their knapsacks for a surprise snack at school.

The Beast's
BREAKFAST PORRIDGE

*I*n one of the most enchanting sequences from Beauty and the Beast, *the two main characters have breakfast together in a cheery chamber suddenly bathed in sunlight after years of darkness. The Beast feels uncomfortable having to use knife, spoon, and fork as opposed to eating with his hands, so to ease his mind, Belle picks up her bowl and brings it to her lips—to the great delight of her host. The poetry of this scene is so enthralling that we were moved to come up with our own dish to add to their table and yours this simple but tasty and nutritious porridge. A bowlful will tame the hungry ogre in you and—who knows?—you, too, may wind up turning into an adorable Prince Charming.*

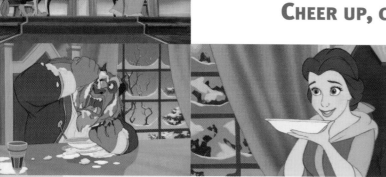

❝ THAT WAS A VERY BRAVE THING YOU DID, MY DEAR. CHEER UP, CHILD. IT'LL TURN OUT ALL RIGHT IN THE END. YOU'LL SEE. OH, LISTEN TO ME. . . JABBERIN' ON WHILE THERE'S A SUPPER TO GET ON THE TABLE! ❞

HOW TO MAKE IT

4 Servings

45 Preparation Time (minutes)

INGREDIENTS

6 oz.	oats, steel cut
1 pinch	salt
1 quart	water
2 tbs.	finely chopped candied ginger root
3 oz.	dried apples, coarsely chopped
1/4 tsp.	cinnamon
	light cream, to taste
	honey, to taste

NUTRITION INFORMATION

Each Serving Contains

Calories	263
Total fat	2 g
Saturated fat	4 g
Carbohydrates	56 g
Sodium	17 mg
Fiber	2 g
Protein	5 g

➡ Place oats in a large saucepan over high heat, stirring well until they smell nutty and take on a light golden color.

➡ Add salt and water, bring to a boil, then reduce to a slow simmer. Cook covered until oats are soft yet chewy, about 30 minutes.

➡ Add candied ginger, dried apples, and cinnamon, remove from heat, and allow to rest no more than 10 minutes before serving.

➡ Place into 4 bowls and serve with light cream and honey, to be spooned on by each person as desired.

NOTES

Other dried fruits may be substituted for apples without changing cooking time. To keep fat content down, use low-fat milk instead of light cream. Honey can be replaced with brown sugar, date sugar, or granulated white sugar.

MENU IDEAS

Serve alongside one of "Jiminy Cricket's Banana Bran Muffins" to really get your morning going.

VARIATIONS

Eliminate the cream—use maple syrup and toasted pecans.

WHAT CHILDREN CAN DO

Kids will enjoy decorating this dish with dried fruit and honey.

Cookie Carnival's
BOYS AND GIRLS

from The Cookie Carnival

eauty pageants are held the world over, in all cultures, but who would have guessed that one was held in Cookie Land way back in 1935? Of course, contestants were cookies and sweets of all kinds. The stars of this brightly colored Silly Symphony are a sweet young waif and the friendly cookie who helps bring out her true beauty. A bit of whipped cream, a touch of frosting, a candied cherry here and there, and the title of Cookie Queen is a cinch. And by her side as King is her cookie helper. We'd like to dedicate this recipe to all the sweet folks who help us to become better people. All of us—even gingerbread cookies—need a friend to bolster our self-esteem now and then.

> ## " THE LOCALS HERE ARE THE SWEETEST
> ## OF ALL. CANDIES, CAKES
> ## AND COOKIES TOO! "

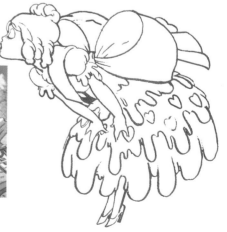

HOW TO MAKE IT

4 Servings

5 Preparation Time (hours)

INGREDIENTS

COOKIE DOUGH

4 tbs.	butter
2 oz.	white sugar
2 oz.	brown sugar
5 oz.	molasses
28 oz.	flour
1 tsp.	baking soda
$1/8$ tsp.	ground cloves
$1/4$ tsp.	ground ginger
$1/2$ tsp.	cinnamon
$1/2$ tsp.	salt
5 tbs.	water
2 oz.	confectioners' sugar

FROSTING

4 oz.	confectioners' sugar
$1/2$ tsp.	vanilla extract
	food coloring, as needed

NUTRITION INFORMATION

Each Serving Contains

Calories	780
Total fat	12 g
Saturated fat	7 g
Carbohydrates	156 g
Sodium	719 mg
Fiber	0 g
Protein	11 g

➡ Preheat oven to 325°F. Line 2 cookie pans with parchment paper. Beat butter until light and fluffy; then add sugars. Cream mixture until there is no sensation of sugar crystals; then slowly beat in molasses.

➡ In a large bowl, sift flour, baking soda, cloves, ginger, cinnamon, and salt. Slowly add dry mixture to butter mixture, incorporating well after each addition. If mixture looks too dry, slowly add water by tablespoons. The dough should have the consistency of modeling clay.

➡ Roll dough in a bit of confectioners' sugar so that it is of uniform texture and free from lumps. Lightly dust cutting board with confectioners' sugar and roll into $1/4$-inch thickness.

➡ Dip gingerbread boy and girl cutters into confectioners' sugar and cut out shapes. Carefully place them on cookie sheets lined with parchment paper.

➡ Bake for 8 to 10 minutes or until firm. Remove from oven and cool on cookie sheets for about 8 minutes before carefully–transferring cookies to cooling racks. Cool 3-4 hours before decorating.

➡ Mix the final measure of confectioners' sugar with vanilla to make a decorating paste, and tint to desired shade with food coloring. Paint and decorate gingerbread boys and girls as desired, accessorizing with little candies while frosting is still wet.

BEVERAGE SUGGESTIONS
Serve with tall glasses of cold milk

WHAT CHILDREN CAN DO

Kids can decorate cookies with tiny candies such as cinnamon red hots, silver dragees, gummi bears, licorice whips, and the like. Don't forget to provide them with lots of damp dishcloths to clean up little messes.

Mary Poppins's

from Mary Poppins

CORN MUFFINS WITH SUN-DRIED CHERRIES

"Practically perfect" is how Mary Poppins defines herself, with a hint of irony. Ah, the governess we all would have wished for— lively and imaginative . . . a touch of her magic and all your problems are whisked away. Though her responsibilities do not include cooking, she makes sure that those in her care eat only healthy foods. Indeed, she'd be proud to serve up these corn muffins with sun-dried cherries. Slightly sweet and tart at the same time, they're the perfect accompaniment to a cup of tea, just right for Sunday brunch and— why not?—even for a meeting at work. They're so quick and easy to prepare that you'll probably have the entire kitchen cleaned up before you can say "Supercalifragilisticexpialidocious."

> **NEVER JUDGE THINGS BY THEIR APPEARANCE. EVEN CARPET BAGS. I'M SURE I NEVER DO!**

HOW TO MAKE IT

12 Servings

30 Preparation Time
(minutes)

INGREDIENTS

12 oz.	flour, sifted
12 oz.	corn meal
1 tb.	baking powder
3/4 tsp.	salt
1	egg, beaten
8 oz.	brown sugar
1/3 cup	skim milk
1/3 cup	maple syrup or honey
1/4 cup	olive oil
3 tbs.	applesauce
4 oz.	dried cherries*

*Sun-dried cherries are available
at most health food stores.

NUTRITION INFORMATION

Each Serving Contains

Calories	297
Total fat	6 g
Saturated fat	1 g
Carbohydrates	59 g
Sodium	179 mg
Fiber	2 g
Protein	4 g

➡ Preheat oven to 350°F. Line two muffin tins (6 muffins each) with paper liners.

➡ Thoroughly mix flour, corn meal, baking powder, and salt in a large bowl.

➡ In a separate bowl, combine egg, brown sugar, skim milk, maple syrup, olive oil, applesauce, and cherries.

➡ Add wet mixture to dry, combining just until there are no traces of dry flour mixture.

➡ Pour into muffin tins and bake until an inserted toothpick comes out clean, 25–30 minutes.

MENU IDEAS

Best served with a little sweet butter and a hot cup of Earl Grey tea.

VARIATIONS

Any type of dried fruit may be used, cutting pieces no larger than 1/2 inch. Sun-dried cherries work best for this recipe, however.

WHAT CHILDREN CAN DO

Kids can mix dry ingredients in one bowl and line muffin pans with paper. They can even use the sun-dried cherries to decorate the tops of muffins with faces before baking.

The Reluctant Dragon's

from The Reluctant Dragon

BREAKFAST WITH THE UPSIDE-DOWN CAKE

he Reluctant Dragon likes to get in touch with his "artistic side" while sipping cups of tea and writing "surrealistic" poetry in the countryside. With his unnatural shyness and careful grooming (love those eyelashes!), rather than actual physical combat, he prefers sharing witty repartee and sharp-tongued barbs with his opponents. One of his most famous poems is even dedicated to an upside-down cake, which means it's only fair to dedicate this scrumptious recipe to him.

> **SWEET LITTLE UPSIDE-DOWN CAKE,
> CARES AND WOES YOU'VE GOT 'EM.
> POOR LITTLE UPSIDE-DOWN CAKE,
> YOUR TOP IS ON YOUR BOTTOM.
> ALAS, LITTLE UPSIDE-DOWN CAKE,
> YOUR TROUBLES NEVER STOP
> BECAUSE, LITTLE UPSIDE-DOWN CAKE,
> YOUR BOTTOM IS ON YOUR TOP.**

HOW TO MAKE IT

4 Servings

75 Preparation Time (minutes)

INGREDIENTS

1 can	pineapple slices, 20 ounces
12 tbs.	unsalted butter
3 oz.	brown sugar
3 oz.	pecan halves
11 oz.	white granulated sugar
2 tsp.	vanilla extract
3	eggs
19 oz.	flour
1⅓ tsps.	baking powder
1⅓ tsps.	baking soda
½ tsp.	salt
11 oz.	sour cream

FROSTING

6 oz.	white chocolate
6 tbs.	unsalted butter
3 oz.	flaked coconut, toasted

NUTRITION INFORMATION

Each Serving Contains

Calories	652
Total fat	38 g
Saturated fat	22 g
Carbohydrates	75 g
Sodium	573 mg
Fiber	2 g
Protein	7 g

TO PREPARE THE PAN

➡ Preheat oven to 325°F. Drain canned pineapple slices; then place on paper towels to dry. Rub ½ ounce of butter over each of two round pans. Divide brown sugar between both pans, pressing down to flatten.

➡ Place 1 pineapple slice onto the center of each pan, and arrange remaining whole slices around it. If they are too large, cut slices in half and make an attractive pattern with the semicircular slices. Place pecan halves in center of pineapple slices, rounded side down.

BATTER

➡ Blend white granulated sugar, the remaining 5 ounces of butter, and vanilla until smooth.

➡ Slowly add eggs, one by one, while mixing. Combine flour, baking powder, baking soda, and salt in a separate bowl.

➡ Alternatively add dry mixture and sour cream to egg mixture.

➡ Now divide batter evenly between the two prepared pans; bake in preheated oven for about 30 minutes, or until an inserted toothpick comes out clean from the center.

➡ Remove and cool on rack for 10 minutes, then lift out of pans and continue to cool until room temperature.

FROSTING

➡ Melt white chocolate and 3 ounces of butter in a glass bowl on top of a double boiler, until smooth, stirring constantly. If using a microwave, stir every 15 seconds until smooth. Once desired smoothness has been attained, add toasted coconut.

ASSEMBLY

➡ Place first cake pineapple side down on a serving platter; then frost the top, smoothing out to the edges. Place second cake pineapple side up on top of frosted layer.

➡ Press down lightly so that frosting oozes out a bit on the sides and layers are firmly attached.

➡ Serve at room temperature.

NOTES

Canned pitted cherries can replace nuts if desired.

VARIATIONS

The recipe may be cut in half for a single-layer cake, perfect for smaller families or those with smaller appetites.

SERVING SUGGESTIONS

Serve this cake just as our dragon does—with a pot of tea and fresh fruit, though avoid using your own belly as a tabletop. If you're still hungry, how about some small tea sandwiches—on the sweet side, of course.

WHAT CHILDREN CAN DO

Kids can prepare pans for the batter, arranging pineapple and nuts in attractive patterns. They may also enjoy mixing the batter.

Mickey Mouse's

from Mickey's Trailer

SPECIAL BREAKFAST

*I*n the well-known 1938 short movie Mickey's Trailer, *Mickey Mouse prepares breakfast for friends Goofy and Donald Duck. His method is truly special, as he "assembles" the meal, using ingredients he gathers from outside his camper's kitchen window. The bizarre result is anything but standard fare, which strangely enough provides inspiration for an original breakfast or brunch of our own. Enjoy this with your family on beautiful, sunny mornings when you wake up feeling particularly happy . . . and slightly deranged.*

" OH, BOY! WHAT A DAY! "

HOW TO MAKE IT

4 Servings

1 Preparation Time (hour)

INGREDIENTS

4 medium	russet potatoes, scrubbed
4 oz.	sour cream
1½ cup	water
4 oz.	instant grits (polenta)
	salt, to taste
6 tbs.	butter
4	ears of corn, cleaned
¼	watermelon, sliced
4 slices	white bread
½ cup	milk
1 pitcher	coffee

➡ Preheat oven to 350°F. Bake potatoes directly on oven racks for about 30 minutes, or until they yield slightly when squeezed.

➡ Lightly whip sour cream; set aside to reach room temperature.

➡ Bring 12 ounces of water to a boil. Slowly add grits (polenta) in a small stream, stirring in the same direction constantly over medium heat until smooth and lump free (8-10 minutes). Add salt to taste and 1 ounce of butter.

➡ Bring a large pot of water to boiling; add salt to taste. Boil corn for about 5 minutes. Meanwhile, slice watermelon and place on a platter. Arrange sliced bread on another platter along with remaining butter. Place milk in a small pitcher to serve alongside coffee.

➡ Remove potatoes from oven when ready, cuting into each one and squeezing the sides to fluff up a bit.

➡ Then place all dishes on the table so everyone can enjoy themselves to a real family-style breakfast.

NUTRITION INFORMATION

Each Serving Contains

Calories	594
Total fat	27 g
Saturated fat	15 g
Carbohydrates	81 g
Sodium	361 mg
Fiber	5 g
Protein	12 g

NOTES

In the film, this meal was way ahead of its time—low in animal protein and saturated fat, but loaded with fruits and vegetables.

MENU IDEAS

You might enjoy some eggs, sunny side up, to round out this meal; try substituting "Mr. Toad's Irish Soda Bread" for white bread.

WHAT CHILDREN CAN DO

Kids can start by scrubbing the potatoes clean with a brush. Then they can also help shuck the corn.

Mr. Toad's IRISH SODA BREAD

from The Adventures of Ichabod and Mr. Toad

The wealthy English landowner Mr. Toad takes pride in his great estate. A lover of all that is new, dangerous, and fast, he is the veteran of a thousand great adventures. But we suspect that the stately old gentleman Toad now prefers the quiet life and often invites his dearest friends, Rat, Mole and Angus Mac Badger, to Toad Hall for a hearty cup of tea. Well, what better occasion than this to offer guests a slice of wholesome and tasty Irish Soda Bread, laced with currants and caraway seeds? Like Mr. Toad, we should all enjoy what life has to offer, which is why things like sharing time with your friends, inviting them to your home, and enjoying goodies like this fresh-baked bread together, are so important.

**❝ HE VOWED ONCE AND FOR ALL . . .
TO FORSAKE THE FOLLIES
OF THE PRIMROSE PATH. ❞**

HOW TO MAKE IT

4	**Servings**
1½	**Preparation Time (hour)**

INGREDIENTS

28 oz.	all-purpose flour
2 oz.	bran
2 oz.	oats, rolled
1 tsp.	salt
1 tsp.	baking powder
12 oz.	buttermilk
1 tb.	caraway seeds
2 oz.	currants

NUTRITION INFORMATION

Each Serving Contains

Calories	257
Total fat	1 g
Saturated fat	5 g
Carbohydrates	52 g
Sodium	362 mg
Fiber	1 g
Protein	9 g

➡ Preheat oven to 400°F. In a large bowl, combine flour, bran, oats, salt, and baking powder, mixing well.

➡ Add buttermilk, caraway seeds, and currants, again mixing well. You may need 2 ounces additional buttermilk if dough is too dry.

➡ Lightly flour a board and knead dough for 1 to 2 minutes.

➡ Place on pregreased baking sheet. Lightly dust top of loaf with flour; then score an *X* on top.

➡ Bake bread for about 45 minutes, or until the top is golden and it sounds hollow when rapped with your knuckles on the bottom. Cool completely before slicing.

NOTES

Toast oats in the oven for 4 to 5 minutes before using for a slightly richer flavor. If you don't have buttermilk, simply add 1 teaspoon of lemon juice to ordinary milk and let stand at room temperature for 10 minutes.

VARIATIONS

Bread may be made into smaller loaves or rolls—remember to reduce baking time.

SERVING SUGGESTIONS

Try your "Irish Soda Bread" lightly buttered, with a hot cup of tea in the afternoon while reading.

WHAT CHILDREN CAN DO

Kids can get involved from beginning to end with this simple, quick bread. Measuring out ingredients becomes a mini math lesson, while kneading and shaping dough provides an amazing opportunity for artistic expression.

The 101 Puppies'

from 101 Dalmatians

KANINE KRUNCHY DOG BISCUITS

*A*ny dog would work up an appetite after watching an episode of Thunderbolt, *the superhero collie.* To keep energy levels up, puppies look to you for sustenance. No ordinary biscuit will do—only one with little beef krunchies on top, made lovingly by "Mom." Surely, a dog biscuit like this would satisfy even little Rolly, the ever hungry pup from 101 Dalmatians. And, given a bit of quiet time, we're sure Pongo and Perdita would enjoy sharing one of these cheesy-flavored treats, basking in the warm glow of the fireplace. Certainly my "little" 110-pound Rottweiler loves them.

❝ YOU CAN BE A CHAMPION, TOO, IF YOU EAT KANINE KRUNCHIES. ❞

HOW TO MAKE IT

12 Servings

1 Preparation Time (hour)

INGREDIENTS

12 oz.	cheddar cheese, shredded
$\frac{1}{4}$ cup	olive oil
$\frac{1}{4}$ cup	milk
2 tsps.	garlic powder
12 oz.	whole-wheat flour
1	egg, beaten
3 cubes	beef bouillon, crushed

➡ Preheat oven to 325°F. Mix cheese and olive oil in a food processor until smooth; then add milk and garlic powder, processing a few more seconds.

➡ Place mixture in a mixing bowl, add flour, and mix until a stiff dough is formed. Roll out to $\frac{1}{4}$-inch thickness and cut bone shapes with a cookie cutter.

➡ Place Krunchies on an ungreased cookie sheet, brush lightly with beaten egg, then sprinkle with crushed bouillon cubes.

➡ Bake for 20 minutes or until edges start to brown. Store at room temperature when cooled.

MENU IDEAS
Even our "puppies" have birthdays, and why should theirs be any different—they are a part of the family, aren't they? So celebrate by starting off with a bowl of warm chicken broth, then a grilled hamburger, and "The 101 Puppies' Kanine Krunchy Dog Biscuits" baked just for the occasion, with your dog's name stamped into each cookie.

WHAT CHILDREN CAN DO

Little hands can help roll and cut the Krunchies with dog bone–shaped cookie cutters as well as writing their dogs' names on the cookies.

Fantasia's PIZZA

from Fantasia

Fantasia *is the cinema triumph of sound and color, as well as a discovery journey to magical or lost worlds: from ancient Greece, where gods and goddesses once roamed, to enchanted forests; from the land of dinosaurs to neoclassical theaters to mountains upon whose peaks forces of good and evil square off.*

We'd like to think that our brightly colored pizza can in some way conjure up the variegated harmony of tastes. You can play with ingredients and colors the way Disney animators juggled all the colors of the rainbow in Fantasia. *And once your pizza has been popped into the oven, let Mickey Mouse and his enchanted brooms clean up the kitchen, while you take a well-deserved rest.*

HOW TO MAKE IT

4	Servings
3	Preparation Time (hours)

INGREDIENTS

2 tbs.	dry yeast
1 tsp.	sugar
2 cups	warm water
36 oz.	flour
4 oz.	semolina flour
1 tsp.	salt
2 tbs.	olive oil

TOPPINGS

2 tbs.	olive oil
1 clove	garlic, minced
3/4 pound	shiitake mushrooms, stemmed, sliced
6 oz.	cherry tomatoes, halved
1/2 lb.	mozzarella cheese, shredded
1/4 lb.	hot peppers, seeded, sliced
1 oz.	feta cheese, crumbled
3 oz.	Kalamata olives, sliced
1/4 cup	extra-virgin olive oil

➡ Dissolve yeast and sugar in water; let stand for 5 minutes. Pour into the bowl of a tabletop mixer with a dough hook.

➡ Slowly mix in the flour (reserving just a bit to knead the dough with) semolina flour, and salt.

➡ Slowly add the remaining flour, mixing for about 10 to 12 minutes or until dough is elastic and very smooth (otherwise you can knead the dough by hand).

➡ Coat the inside of a large mixing bowl with olive oil; then add dough, turning to coat lightly. Cover with a dish-cloth or plastic wrap and let rise until doubled in bulk, about $1^1/_2$ hours at room temperature; or place in the bottom of your refrigerator overnight for more flavorful dough.

➡ While dough is "resting," heat a nonstick pan, sauté olive oil, garlic, and mushrooms 10-12 minutes or until they sizzle loudly in the pan. Remove from pan and hold at room temperature.

WHAT CHILDREN CAN DO

This is a great activity for children! From the preparation of the dough to the assembly of the pizza, they can get totally involved. Toppings may be modified to accommodate kids' tastes.

HOW TO MAKE IT

VARIATIONS
Serve this pizza topped with four centric rings of ingredients, so each slice contains all four flavors in separate sections.

NOTES
Use whole-wheat flour in place of half the regular flour for a heartier crust. Try replacing mushrooms with marinated artichoke hearts—drained, of course.

➡ Now punch the dough down—either the next morning or after $1^1/_2$ hours once it has doubled in size. Reshape into 2 balls and refrigerate until ready to use. Remove dough from refrigerator and let stand for about 20 minutes before shaping. Preheat oven to 500°F. If possible, use a pizza stone for crispier crust. Lightly dust the work surface and your hands with flour.

➡ Stretch out a ball of dough, using your fingers and the back of your knuckles, to a 14-inch circle with a raised "crust" around the outer edge. Place dough on a pizza peel also lightly dusted with flour or semolina or on the back of a cookie pan sprinkled with corn meal.

➡ Starting from the outside working in, top with concentric rings of sautéed mushrooms, cherry tomatoes, mozzarella cheese, sliced hot peppers, and finally a circle of feta cheese in the middle, with sliced olives on top. Slide pie very quickly off the peel onto the hot pizza stone and bake for about 10 minutes, checking after about 8 minutes. If necessary, turn pizza so that it browns evenly.

➡ Continue with the next dough ball in the same manner. Pizza is done when nicely browned around the crust and the bottom is attractively colored. Remove from oven and drizzle with about 1 ounce of extra-virgin olive oil. Allow to cool for about 5 minutes before slicing and serving.

The Hundred Acre Wood's

from The Many Adventures of Winnie the Pooh

CARROT BREAD

4	Servings
1½	Preparation Time (hours)

INGREDIENTS

12 oz.	carrots (about 2½ large carrots)
8 oz.	brown sugar
4 oz.	buttermilk*
½ cup	olive oil
1 tb.	vanilla extract
2	eggs, beaten
11 oz.	flour
½ tbs.	baking soda
1 tsp.	cinnamon
⅛ tsp.	salt

*For buttermilk, see Notes on page 205.

NUTRITION INFORMATION

Each Serving Contains

Calories	238
Total fat	12 g
Saturated fat	2 g
Carbohydrates	30 g
Sodium	252 mg
Fiber	1 g
Protein	3 g

Preheat oven to 325°F. Lightly grease a 2-pound loaf pan. Peel and grate carrots; set aside.

➡ In a large mixing bowl, combine sugar, buttermilk, oil, vanilla, and eggs. Add flour to grated carrots and mix thoroughly. Then add baking soda, cinnamon, and salt.

➡ Combine wet mixture and dry ingredients until no dry flour is visible; then pour into greased loaf pan. Avoid overmixing, or bread will be tough.

➡ Bake in preheated oven for 40 minutes or until a toothpick inserted in the middle comes out clean. Cool for 20 minutes; then remove from pan.

➡ Complete cooling on a wire rack before slicing, to avoid crumbling.

NOTES

Four ounces of roasted walnuts and/or 4 ounces of raisins may be added to the batter, along with carrots. If adding both, reduce grated carrots by 4½ ounces.

SERVING SUGGESTIONS

Serve lightly toasted with butter and honey.

WHAT CHILDREN CAN DO

Older kids can grate carrots and help mix the batter.

❝ WHY DID I *EVER* INVITE THAT BEAR TO LUNCH? ❞

Fantasia 2000's
PIZZA

If you liked Pizza Fantasia, then Pizza Fantasia 2000 is sure to be a hit. For this updated version, the most classic ingredients are boldly teamed up with less traditional toppings.

The stupendous alchemy of images, colors, and sounds that makes the film a masterpiece for all time is truly based on an ingenious array of contrasts—the perfect inspiration for a tasty, sweet-and-spicy, variegated pizza. Though the combination may seem a bit bizarre, keep in mind that culinary fantasy is unlimited.

HOW TO MAKE IT

4 Servings

4 Preparation Time (hours)

INGREDIENTS

2 tbs.	dry yeast
1 tsp.	sugar
2 cups	warm water
36 oz.	flour
4 oz.	semolina flour
1 tsp.	salt
2 tbs.	olive oil

TOPPINGS

10	mushrooms, quartered
$1/4$	red onion, thickly sliced
$1/4$ cup	olive oil
1 clove	garlic, minced
$1/4$ lb.	chicken sausage, spicy, sliced
$1/4$ lb.	plum tomatoes, seeded and crushed
1 tb.	rosemary, chopped
$1/4$ tsp.	salt
2 oz.	Parmesan cheese, shredded
2 oz.	almonds, crushed
2 oz.	blue cheese, crumbled
3 oz.	mozzarella cheese, shredded
1 bunch	arugala, washed and ripped
2 tbs.	extra-virgin olive oil
2 oz.	peas, fresh

➡ Dissolve yeast and sugar in water, let stand for 5 minutes. Pour into the bowl of a tabletop mixer with a dough hook.

➡ Slowly mix in the flour (reserving just a bit to knead the dough with) semolina flour, and salt.

➡ Slowly add the remaining flour, mix for 10 to 12 minutes or until dough is elastic and very smooth (otherwise you can knead the dough by hand).

➡ Coat the inside of a large mixing bowl with olive oil, then add dough. Turn to coat lightly and cover with a dish towel or plastic wrap, letting dough rise until doubled in bulk, about $1^1/_2$ hours at room temperature; or place in the bottom of your refrigerator overnight for more flavorful dough.

➡ Toss mushrooms with onions, 1 ounce of olive oil, and garlic. Set aside.

➡ Slice chicken sausage. Set aside. Combine tomatoes, rosemary, remaining olive oil, and salt. Marinate at room temperature.

➡ Now punch the dough down—either the next morning or after $1^1/_2$ hours once it is doubled in size. Reshape into 2 balls and refrigerate until ready to use. Remove dough from refrigerator and let stand for about 20 minutes before shaping.

MENU SUGGESTIONS

Glasses of "Heroes' Herculade," lots of napkins, and "Daisy Duck's Orange-Flavored Brownies" would round this meal out nicely, while watching your favorite movie.

WHAT CHILDREN CAN DO

With this recipe, pizza-making may well become one of your kids' favorite sports. They can even use the toppings they like best.

NOTES

Use whole-wheat flour in place of half the all-purpose flour for a heartier crust.

VARIATIONS

The "capriccioso"-style pizza is made up of four different quadrants each with its own topping. For more fun, cut down the middle of each section so that each slice contains two different toppings.

HOW TO MAKE IT

➡ Preheat oven to 500°F. If possible, use a pizza stone for crispier crust. Lightly dust work surface and your hands with flour.

➡ Stretch out a ball of dough with your fingers and the back of your knuckles to a 14-inch circle with a raised "crust" around the outer edge. Place dough on a pizza peel, also lightly dusted with flour or semolina (or use the back of a cookie pan sprinkled with cornmeal).

➡ Sprinkle Parmesan cheese over one quarter of the pizza; top with mixed marinated vegetables. Cover the next quarter with almonds; top with blue cheese. On the third quarter place slices of chicken sausage; sprinkle lightly with mozzarella cheese. Spoon tomato mixture onto the final quarter.

➡ Slide pizza very quickly onto hot pizza stone and bake for about 10 minutes, checking after about 8 minutes. If necessary, turn pizza so that it browns evenly. Pizza is done when nicely browned around the crust and the bottom is attractively colored.

➡ Remove from oven, place arrugala over chicken section, allowing it to wilt. Sprinkle peas over the section with the marinated mushroom mixture, allowing the heat of the pizza to "cook" the peas. Drizzle all with about 1 ounce of extra-virgin olive oil. Repeat procedure with second dough ball. Cool for 5 minutes or so before slicing and serving.

Jiminy Cricket's
BANANA BRAN MUFFINS

from Pinocchio

12 Servings

45 Preparation Time (minutes)

INGREDIENTS

12 oz.	flour
4 oz.	bran
2 tsp.	baking powder
1/4 tsp.	salt
4 oz.	raisins, seedless
4 oz.	sunflower seeds, toasted
2	egg whites
2 tbs.	sugar
3	large ripe bananas
6 oz.	applesauce
1 tsp.	vanilla extract

Preheat oven to 375°F. Lightly grease 2 muffin tins, 6 muffins each.

➡ In a large bowl, combine flour, bran, baking powder, salt, raisins, and sunflower seeds.

➡ In a separate bowl, combine egg whites and sugar. Add bananas, applesauce, and vanilla, beating until there are no lumps. Mix wet and dry ingredients until combined, and avoiding overmixing.

➡ Spoon into paper-lined muffin tins. Sprinkle tops with refined sugar (white) and bake 15-22 minutes until golden brown on top, or until an inserted toothpick comes out clean.

> **NOW, YOU SEE, THE WORLD IS FULL OF TEMPTATIONS. TEMPTATIONS? YEP. TEMPTATIONS.**

NUTRITION INFORMATION

Each Serving Contains

Calories	137
Total fat	2 g
Saturated fat	0.3 g
Monounsaturated fat	0.4 g
Sodium	116 mg
Fiber	2 g
Protein	3 g

NOTES
Freeze the baked muffins then defrost and reheat when temptation comes knocking at your door.

VARIATIONS
Other dried fruits may be used instead of raisins, such as cranberries, blueberries, or cherries. Replace sunflower seeds with pecans, walnuts, or slightly crushed almonds.

SERVING SUGGESTIONS
Serve muffins with fresh fruit and a hot beverage, for a low-fat meal rich in complex carbohydrates.

WHAT CHILDREN CAN DO
Little hands can help by mashing up the bananas. Use ripe brown ones—they're easier to mash and sweeter to eat.

Donald Duck's

from Chef Donald *and* Three for Breakfast

PANCAKES AND WAFFLES

*I*n the short movies Chef Donald *(1941) and* Three for Breakfast *(1948), Donald Duck attempts to prepare pancakes and waffles, with ghastly results! In the first, had he been paying attention, he certainly would have used flour in the batter instead of "rubber cement"; in the second, Donald's house is left a shambles after sweet-toothed guests Chip and Dale get through with it. With these recipes, your pancakes and waffles are sure to turn out perfect, so don't let Donald's frightening culinary adventures keep you from enjoying a robust and nutritious breakfast with your family.*

"WHAT'S THE BIG IDEA?! OH-OH!"

HOW TO MAKE IT

4 Servings

1 Preparation Time (hour)

INGREDIENTS

PANCAKES

1 cup	buttermilk*
1	egg
3 tbs.	butter, melted
4 oz.	flour
1 tb.	sugar
1/4 tsp.	salt
1 tsp.	baking soda
	olive oil

*For buttermilk see Notes on page 205.

NUTRITION INFORMATION

Each Serving Contains

Calories	231
Total fat	10 g
Saturated fat	6 g
Carbohydrates	28 g
Sodium	613 mg
Fiber	0 g
Protein	7 g

PANCAKES

➡ Preheat oven to 200°F. Mix buttermilk, egg, and melted butter in one bowl, and combine remaining ingredients in a separate large bowl.

➡ Pour dry ingredients into wet ingredients and mix. Allow batter to rest for at least 30 minutes. Since batter may rest for up to 9 hours, you may prepare it the night before and refrigerate.

➡ Heat a nonstick griddle on the stove (test temperature with a few drops of water—when they dance and evaporate quickly, your griddle is hot enough). Coat hot griddle with oil, by dabbling a bit on with a paper towel. Do not use too much oil.

➡ With a ladle, pour batter in small circles onto hot griddle; cook for 2 to 3 minutes before flipping. You should flip pancakes only when bubbles form on top, leaving holes as they pop, and when bottoms are evenly browned.

➡ Continue until all are done, keeping prepared pancakes warm in the oven as you go.

VARIATIONS

Once batter has been poured onto griddle, berries, chocolate chips, or thin slices of banana may be dropped onto them as the pancakes cook.

SERVING SUGGESTIONS

Thin batter slightly by adding more buttermilk; then prepare pancakes as above. They should be thinner than regular pancakes, though not as thin as crepes. Roll them around mixed berries and top with whipped cream for a quick dessert.

WHAT CHILDREN CAN DO

They can help mix the batter and place "add-ons," such as berries, chocolate chips, and banana slices on the cakes as the pancakes cook.

217

HOW TO MAKE IT

VARIATIONS

For a heartier waffle, replace half the all-purpose flour with whole-wheat flour. Do not add berries or fruits to the batter, as they may cause waffles to stick to waffle iron.

MENU IDEAS

The perfect accompaniments to this dish are crisp bacon, moist sausages, and warm maple syrup.

WAFFLES

➡ Mix dry and wet ingredients, as in pancakes. Heat waffle iron (test temperature with a few drops of water—when they dance and evaporate quickly, your waffle iron is hot enough).

➡ Grease the waffle iron the waffle iron with olive oil and pour about ⅓ cup of the batter onto the iron. Press top down gently to distribute batter evenly.

➡ If using a conventional waffle iron on the stove, flip the iron when one side of waffle looks golden brown.Cook the other side a few minutes, also until golden brown. If using an electric model, cook both sides simultaneously, making cooking time shorter. There is no need to flip.

4 Servings

1 Preparation Time (hour)

INGREDIENTS

WAFFLES

16 oz.	flour
3 tbs.	sugar
1 tb.	baking powder
1 tsp.	salt
2	eggs
4 tbs.	butter, melted
2 cups	milk
	olive oil

*D*rinks

Heroes' HERCULADE

from Hercules

Hercules is so gloriously hailed by the people of Thebes that you might mistake him for a Hollywood star. Between one feat of strength and courage and the next— oh, the usual stuff, defeating the Minotaur here, Medusa there, plugging up an erupting volcano, and so on—he even manages to do a testimonial for an energizing drink named in his honor. Here, then, is a beverage of royal hue and effervescence to help make you a champion among champions, although we can't promise that you'll develop a square jawline or bulging muscles like Herc's. But as Phil, Herc's personal trainer, continually reminds his boy, developing strong convictions and solid ideals is also important.

> ❝ **UH, EXACTLY HOW DO YOU BECOME A TRUE HERO?** ❞

HOW TO MAKE IT

4 Servings

15 Preparation Time (minutes)

INGREDIENTS

¹/₂	orange
4	mint sprigs
1 pint	purple grape juice
1 pint	ginger ale
1 pint	club soda

NUTRITION INFORMATION

Each Serving Contains

Calories	125
Total fat	0 g
Saturated fat	0 g
Sodium	37 g
Carbohydrates	31 g
Fiber	0 g
Protein	5 g

➡ Cut ¹/₂ orange into 4 wedges. Fill four large glasses with ice and garnish each with a sprig of mint and orange wedge along rim.

➡ Pour remaining ingredients into a pitcher, stir quickly, then serve in garnished glasses.

VARIATIONS

This drink may also be made with cranberry juice.

SERVING SUGGESTIONS

A great punch to serve at birthday parties, as an alternative to sodas.

MENU IDEAS

Very refreshing when served during a hot summer barbecue.

WHAT CHILDREN CAN DO

Kids can make this from start to finish. Older ones, with just a bit of supervision, can cut orange wedges.

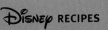

Rafiki's
from The Lion King

COCONUT DRINK

afiki the shaman baboon is keeper of all the savannah's many secrets. It is his job to present newborn Simba to the throng of animals that gathers to celebrate his birth, and he is also the one to convince the runaway youth to return to Pride Land and assume his rightful place as leader. Such a peculiar and important character merits a truly special recipe in his honor, which is why we've chosen this luscious cocktail, rich in the fragrances of Africa—its main ingredient could only be coconut. And if something from your own past is still haunting you, remember the words of the wise old ape: "Oh, yes, the past can hurt. But the way I see it, you can either run from it or learn from it. . . ."

66 ASANTE SANA. SQUASH BANANA.
WE WE NUGU.
MI MI APANA 99

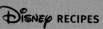

HOW TO MAKE IT

4	Servings
30	Preparation Time (minutes)

INGREDIENTS

4	coconuts, green young type
4 tsps.	sugar
1	lime, juice only
1	banana, peeled and chunked
1 piece	gingerroot, 1/4 inch thick
6 oz.	pineapple juice
1	lime, quartered
1 sheet	edible gold (optional)

NUTRITION INFORMATION

Each Serving Contains

Calories	219
Total fat	14 g
Saturated fat	12 g
Sodium	10 mg
Carbohydrates	25 g
Fiber	5 g
Protein	2 g

➡ Carefully cut off the top of each coconut with a very sharp knife to create nifty coconut shell tumblers.

➡ Pour juice from all coconuts through a strainer into a bowl.

➡ In a blender combine coconut juice, sugar, lime juice, banana, gingerroot, and pineapple juice until smooth. Add 6 ounces of ice and continue to process until smooth.

➡ Pour back into coconut shell tumblers. Garnish with a long straw and a wedge of lime.

➡ Optional garnish: edible gold crushed into a fine powder and sprinkled on top of your drinks, the way Rafiki anoints Prince Simba's brow with ceremonial dust.

MENU IDEAS

Accompany this drink with a platter of "Lumiere's Appetizers" and music—a great way to start your next party.

VARIATIONS

Add 4 scoops of vanilla ice crem when blending this drink for a truly adult smoothie.

WHAT CHILDREN CAN DO

Little hands can help to peel and chunk the bananas as well as squeeze the lime for the juice.

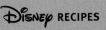

Saludos Amigos' GAZPACHO

In the Saludos Amigos *episode "Aquarela do Brasil"* *(1943), Donald Duck meets up with his friend José Carioca for* *the first time. José is quick to fill the visitor in on the local* *customs and traditions. In a memorable sequence, the adorable* *parrot offers unsuspecting Donald a taste of South American* *hooch,* cachaca, *which he downs in a single gulp. But have no* *fear, our gazpacho is a nonalcoholic beverage that won't explode* *in your stomach and leave you gasping for air like poor Donald.* *A tribute to the astonishing land of spicy rhythms and tastes* *where it originated, this refreshing drink makes a super-starter* *for a summer lunch or a fine dinner appetizer—the perfect way* *to get your daily dose of vegetables in a bowl. And you won't* *even need a fork to eat them!*

❝ DONALD! NOW YOU HAVE THE SPIRIT OF THE SAMBA! ❞

HOW TO MAKE IT

4 Servings

30 Preparation Time (minutes)

INGREDIENTS

¹/₂	cucumber, peeled, and seeded
¹/₂	red bell pepper, cored and seeded
¹/₂	green bell pepper, cored and seeded
¹/₂	red onion, peeled
1 rib	celery, peeled
8	plum tomatoes, peeled and seeded
1 quart	low-salt tomato juice
2 oz.	extra-virgin olive oil
2 oz.	red-wine vinegar
¹/₂ tsp.	salt
¹/₂ tsp.	black pepper

➡ Finely chop all vegetables into very small cubes, place in a stainless steel or glass bowl. Add tomato juice, oil, and vinegar, plus salt and black pepper.

➡ Mix well and taste for seasonings.

➡ Chill for several hours before serving.

NUTRITIONAL INFORMATION

Each Serving Contains

Calories	234
Total fat	15 g
Saturated fat	2 g
Sodium	321 g
Carbohydrates	26 g
Fiber	6 g
Protein	5 g

SERVING SUGGESTIONS

In Spain, gazpacho is often served with ice cubes and croutons for added ice-cold texture.

VARIATIONS

Use any of your favorite fresh and crisp vegetables for a real summer treat. Make this into a hearty entrée by adding cooked shrimp, crab meat, or boneless fish and cold steamed potatoes, for a lovely cool "stew."

MENU IDEAS

Serve this in small cups on a hot day before a platter of "Three Caballeros' Vegetarian Burritos."

WHAT CHILDREN CAN DO

Kids can help to make fun shapes out of the cucumber or peppers to decorate the cups of gazpacho, with parental supervision of course. They can also mix and stir everything.

Walt Disney's RECIPES

All the best-loved stars from the cavalcade of Disney characters—like Mickey Mouse and Donald Duck, Snow White and the Little Mermaid, and many, many more—bring to life this special collection of recipes. To top it all off, we've even included a pair of gastronomic gems created by none other than Walt Disney himself. The original manuscripts shown below were found in the archives of the Walt Disney Studios in Burbank, California. While the book they were meant for was never completed, they provide a fitting end to Disney Recipes.

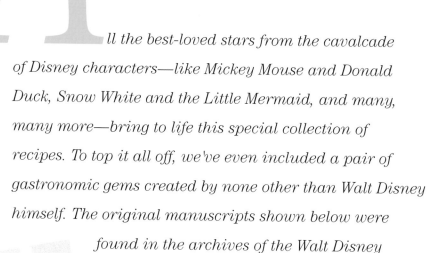

CHILI & BEANS

2 lbs. coarse ground beef
2 onions, sliced
2 cloves garlic
½ C. oil
1 C. chopped celery
1 tsp. chili powder, or to taste
1 tsp. paprika
1 tsp. dry mustard
1 lg. can solid pack tomatoes
Salt
2 lbs. dry pink beans
For spicier chili, add a pinch of the following: coriander, tumeric, chili seeds, fennel, cloves, cinnamon, dry ginger, small yellow mexican chili pepper.

Soak beans overnight in cold water. Drain. Add water to cover 2" over beans & simmer with onions until tender (about 4 hrs.) Meanwhile, prepare sauce by browning meat & minced garlic in oil. Add remaining items & simmer 1 hr. When beans are tender, add sauce & simmer ½ hr. Serves 6-8.

Walt Disney

BROWNED ROAST BEEF HASH

Prime rib of beef chopped fine.
1 onion chopped fine, smothered with butter & fried
1 med. potato chopped in very small pieces
Mix together & add 1 C. beef stock. Put in pan in 350° oven 1 hr. Form it like an omelette, then place in frying pan & brown. Serve with 1 egg on top.

Walt Disney

THE RECIPES

INDEX

FILMOGRAPHY

FULL-LENGTH MOVIES

Snow White and the Seven Dwarfs (1937):
Snow White's Winter Vegetable Soup
Snow White's Gooseberry Pie

Pinocchio (1940):
Figaro's Trout in Crazy Water
*Jiminy Cricket's Banana
  Bran Muffins*
*Pinocchio's Farfalle with Leeks
  and Sausages*
*Stromboli's Penne with Grilled
  Vegetables*

Fantasia (1940):
Fantasia's Pizza

The Reluctant Dragon (1941):
*The Reluctant Dragon's Breakfast
  with the Upside-Down Cake*

Dumbo (1941):
*Dumbo's Roasted Peanut Pie
  with Chocolate*

Bambi (1942):
*Bambi and Thumper's
  Green Goddess Dressing*

Saludos Amigos (1943):
Saludos Amigos' Gazpacho

The Three Caballeros (1945):
Three Caballeros' Vegetarian Burritos

Make Mine Music (1946):
*Willie the Whale's Pappardelle
  with Shrimp*
Make Mine Music's Double Soup

Fun and Fancy Free (1947):
Willie the Giant's Mixed Sandwich
Fun and Fancy Free's Ratatouille

Melody Time (1948):
*Pecos Bill's Grilled Rib-Eye Steak
  with Red-Eye Gravy*
*Melody Time Cold's Poached Shrimp
  with Melons*
Johnny Appleseed's Apple Pie

**The Adventures of Ichabod
  and Mr. Toad (1949):**
*Ichabod's Roast Turkey
  with Giblet Gravy*
Mr. Toad's Irish Soda Bread

So Dear to My Heart (1949):
"So Dear to My Heart" Pasta

Cinderella (1950):
Cinderella's Herb and Egg White Soup

Alice in Wonderland (1951):
Alice's Warm Mushroom Salad
The Cheshire Cat's Marinated Fish Salad
*The Mad Hatter and March Hare's
  Cheesecake*
*The Walrus and Carpenter's Fresh
  Oyster Salad*

Peter Pan (1953) :
Captain Hook's Codfish Fillet
Peter Pan's Crispy Spinach
  with "Pixie Dust"
Tinker Bell's Golden Herb Melange

Lady and the Tramp (1955):
Lady and the Tramp's Spaghetti Bella Notte
Si and Am's Appetizers

Sleeping Beauty (1959):
Fauna's Birthday Cake
King Hubert's Veal Roast with Apricots and
  Thyme
Princess Aurora's Berried
  Honey Butter

101 Dalmatians (1961):
The 101 Puppies' Kanine Krunchy
  Dog Biscuits

The Sword in the Stone (1963):
Madam Mim's Dragon Soup
Merlin's Magical Broth
Sir Ector's Whiskey-Glazed Ham

Mary Poppins (1964):
Mary Poppins's Corn Muffins
  with Sun-Dried Cherries

The Many Adventures of Winnie the Pooh (1966):
The Hundred Acre Wood's Carrot Bread
Winnie the Pooh's No-Bake Honey Cookies

The Jungle Book (1967):
Baloo's Jungle Ambrosia Salad
King Louie's Bananas
  with Honey and Coconut
Mowgli's Mixed Vegetable Salad

The Aristocats (1970):
The Aristocats' "Crème de la Crème"
  with Milk and Honey
The Scat Cat Band's Crispy Fried Sole Fillets
  with Raw Tomato Sauce

Bedknobs and Broomsticks (1971):
Mrs. Price's Cabbage Buds
  with Braised Nettles

Robin Hood (1973):
Maid Marian's Blackberry Pie
Robin Hood's Creamy Carrot Soup

Pete's Dragon (1977):
Elliott's Caramelized Red Apples

The Rescuers (1977)/The Rescuers Down Under (1990):
The Rescuers' Sweet Potato Pie with Cheese

The Fox and the Hound (1981):
Widow Tweed's Cheddar Soup
  with Herbed Crisps

The Black Cauldron (1985):
The Black Cauldron's Forest Soup

The Great Mouse Detective (1986):
Basil's Smoked Salmon Tartare

Oliver & Company (1988):
Oliver & Company's Dry-Roasted Chicken

The Little Mermaid (1989):
Ariel's "Under the Sea" Tempura
Louis's Seafood Chowder

Beauty and the Beast (1991):
The Beast's Breakfast Porridge
Lumiere's Appetizers

Aladdin (1992):
Aladdin's Rice Pudding
Genie's Free-Form Lasagna

The Lion King (1994):
Pumbaa and Timon's Potatoes
 with Caramelized Onions
Simba's Seared Fillet of Beef
Rafiki's Coconut Drink

Pocahontas (1995):
Pocahontas's Savory
Indian Corn Pudding

The Hunchback of Notre Dame (1996):
Esmeralda's Turkey Piccata
Quasimodo's Multicolored Cabbage Salad
 and Chicken

Hercules (1997):
Philoctetes' Onion Marmalade
 with Raisins
Heroes' Herculade

Mulan (1998):
Mulan's Mahogany Chicken
Mushu's Egg Rolls and Juk

Tarzan (1999):
Tarzan and Jane's Grilled Tropical Fruits
 with Passion Fruit Coulis

Fantasia/2000 (2000):
Fantasia 2000's Pizza

The Emperor's New Groove (2000):
Kuzco's Spinach Puffs

The Tigger Movie (2000):
Tigger's Frozen Dark Chocolate Orange
 Mousse

Atlantis: The Lost Empire (2001):
Cookie's Special Chili

Lilo & Stitch (2002):
Lilo & Stitch's Hawaiian Sandwich

Treasure Planet (2002):
Treasure Planet's Astral Soup

SILLY SYMPHONIES

The Night Before Christmas (1933):
Santa's Cookies

Three Little Pigs (1933):
The Three Little Pigs' Potato Pancakes
 with Applesauce

The Grasshopper and the Ants (1934):
The Grasshopper and the Ants' Lentil Soup

The Wise Little Hen (1934):
Wise Little Hen's Roasted Corn Soup

The Cookie Carnival (1935):
Cookie Carnival's Boys and Girls

The Golden Touch (1935):
King Midas's Hamburger Stuffed
 with Golden Onions

Three Little Wolves (1936):
The Big Bad Wolf's Dream: Barbecued
Spareribs with Blackberry Sauce

SHORT MOVIES

Shanghaied (1934):
Peg Leg Pete's Seared Swordfish
with Mint Bread-Crumb Sauce

Donald's Nephews (1938):
Huey, Dewey, and Louie's Chocolate Pie

Mickey's Trailer (1938):
Mickey Mouse's Special Breakfast

Donald's Cousin Gus (1939):
Gus the Goose's Spaghetti with Peas

Chef Donald (1941)/Three for
Breakfast (1948):
Donald Duck's Pancakes and Waffles

Mickey's Birthday Party (1942):
Goofy's Birthday Cake

Cold Turkey (1951):
Pluto's Cold Roast Turkey Breast

Trick or Treat (1952):
Witch Hazel's Pumpkin Pie

Various:
Chip and Dale's Corn "Chips"
Clarabelle Cow's Tagliatelle

Daisy Duck's Orange-Flavored Brownies
Horace Horsecollar's Cool Pasta
with "Salsa Fresca"
Humphrey the Bear's Sandwich
Minnie Mouse's Pasta with Three Cheeses
Uncle Scrooge's Golden Risotto

This book was made possible by the unwavering support of co-workers, friends and colleagues. Thank you so much!

We would also like to thank the good folks at Disney Libri Italy, especially Annachiara Tassan for her enthusiasm and supreme guidance, and Cristina Romanelli for her patience, passion and editorial leadership.

Wendy Lefkon at Disney Editions in New York for her belief and support in all our efforts.

Ken Shue, Tim Lewis, Marina Migliavacca, and Camilla Vedove at Global Operations Disney Publishing Worldwide, who with their friendly and efficient manner, helped to locate the animation drawings that enhance these pages.

Vivian Procopio at the Walt Disney Animation Research Library for her contributions in research.

The Colavita Companies, Industria Alimentare Colavita S.p.a., Oleifici Colavita S.p.a., and Colavita USA L.L.C., for their financial support of this project, as well as for their belief in the link between food, animation, life, and love.

Claudio Garofalo for his expertise in acquiring images digitally.

Mariella Rossomandi for her support in the area of digital graphics.

Ira L. Meyer
Marcello Garofalo

Ira would also like to extend his special thanks to:

JoJo for her help in testing recipes, her constant smile, and her ability to make me blush.

Richard for my photo on the back cover as well as his continued and unwavering support.

My "regulars" who knew that "testing Monday" was the day to visit me in the kitchen for tasty tidbits with unbiased answers in return.

My kitchen staff who put up with my craziness during the creation of this book.

Rocky and Jennifer who offered honest opinions and suggestions.

And last but far from least, my sister Rachel who believed in me from the get go, always reminding me to be true to my tastes and my dream.